THE ULTIMATE LLC AND S-CORPORATION BEGINNER'S GUIDE

The most Update Guide on How to Form, Manage, Grow your LLC & S-Corp and Save on Taxes as a Small Business Owner. (PATH-TO-SUCCESS)

REID C. WILLIAMS

Reid C. Williams

THE ULTIMATE LLC AND S-CORPORATION BEGINNER'S GUIDE

COPYRIGHT

Reid C. Williams
THE ULTIMATE LLC AND S-CORPORATION BEGINNER'S GUIDE

Reid C. Williams

THE ULTIMATE LLC AND S-CORPORATION BEGINNER'S GUIDE

TABLE OF CONTENTS

Reid C. Williams
THE ULTIMATE LLC AND S-CORPORATION BEGINNER'S GUIDE

LLC BEGINNER'S GUIDE

Reid C. Williams

THE ULTIMATE LLC AND S-CORPORATION BEGINNER'S GUIDE

INTRODUCTION

When venturing into the world of business, understanding the area of Limited Liability Companies (LLCs) is a logical beginning point. LLCs, or Limited Liability Companies, are a versatile and appealing company form that integrates the advantages of both corporations and partnerships while affording liability protection to its members. This beginner's book is aimed at unraveling the complicated tapestry of LLCs, presenting a full analysis of their workings, benefits, and possible hazards. Throughout this trip, we'll go into understanding the underlying mechanics of LLCs, analyzing the advantages and drawbacks of founding one, and determining if forming an LLC corresponds with your business ambitions.

Moreover, we'll investigate the variegated terrain of LLCs, deconstructing numerous varieties such as Member-Managed and Manager-Managed LLCs, Domestic and Foreign LLCs, Professional Limited Liability Companies, and Series LLCs. Understanding these variances is crucial to adjust the structure to your company's demands.

This handbook isn't simply a theoretical investigation; it's a path to action. We'll cover the critical procedures involved in beginning an LLC, offering insights into the vital features such as name, appointing a registered agent, preparing and submitting appropriate papers, and creating the operating agreement to create the basis for a healthy corporate organization.

Additionally, we'll walk through the labyrinth of frequent problems faced when creating and maintaining an LLC, educating you on how to prevent these blunders. From picking the correct entity and state for registration to maintaining compliance and segregating corporate and personal finances, we'll provide you with the expertise to traverse the complicated terrain of LLC administration.

But this journey isn't only about the establishment and administration of an LLC; it's also about making educated judgments. We'll assess the prospect of converting current companies into LLCs and cover accounting concepts, taxation, and the complexities of filing taxes as an LLC.

This book isn't just about conveying knowledge; it's about enabling you to make well-informed choices, handle problems, and develop a strong foundation for your commercial pursuits. So, let's go on this educational voyage into the world of Limited Liability Companies together.

CHAPTER ONE: EXPOSITION OF LLC

1.1 What Exactly are LLCs and How Do They Work?

Limited Liability Companies (LLCs) are a unique hybrid company form that amalgamates the advantages of both corporations and partnerships while affording liability protection to its members.

Understanding the workings of LLCs is crucial to appreciating their relevance in the commercial world.

At its foundation, an LLC is a legal company that guarantees limited responsibility to its owners, known as members. This implies that the members' assets are often safeguarded from the company's liabilities, insulating them from certain legal and financial duties of the corporation. However, this liability protection could have significant restrictions, notably in circumstances involving personal commitments or serious wrongdoing.

One of the distinguishing aspects of an LLC is its flexibility in terms of administration and taxes. Unlike corporations with inflexible hierarchies, LLCs provide alternative management structures, enabling members to select between member-managed or manager-managed settings. This freedom extends to taxes, as LLCs may decide to be taxed as a partnership, corporation, or even as a sole proprietorship in the case of single-member LLCs.

LLCs function under an operating agreement, which acts as a guiding document detailing the company's management structure, member roles, profit distribution, and decision-making procedures. This internal document aids in controlling the activities of the LLC, maintaining clarity, and minimizing any disagreements among members.

Furthermore, the everlasting existence of an LLC, independent of changes in ownership or management, sets it apart from sole proprietorships or partnerships, which can face dissolution upon specific occurrences, such as the departure of a partner.

The functioning and governance of LLCs vary from state to state owing to varied legal requirements and laws. Understanding these state-specific subtleties is critical when creating and administering an LLC since compliance with state regulations is crucial for retaining the company's legal existence.

In essence, LLCs provide a diverse and safe corporate structure that combines liability protection, operational flexibility, and tax benefits. This unique mixture of traits makes LLCs an appealing alternative for entrepreneurs seeking a safe but agile company form.

1.2 The Pros and Cons of Establishing a Limited Liability Company in General

Embarking on the adventure of creating an LLC comes with a list of perks and concerns. Let's look into the positives and downsides of launching this specific company structure:

Pros:

Limited Liability: The greatest benefit is the protection of personal assets. Members are typically not individually accountable for the debts and liabilities of the LLC.

Flexible Management: LLCs provide adjustable structures, allowing for multiple management arrangements depending on the interests and requirements of the members.

Pass-Through Taxes: LLCs generally enjoy pass-through taxes, meaning income and losses are transmitted straight to the members, avoiding double taxation often associated with corporations.

Operational Autonomy: Compared to corporations, LLCs have fewer formalities and paperwork obligations, allowing greater operational autonomy.

Credibility: Forming an LLC may boost the credibility of your firm since it displays a dedication to formalizing and legitimizing your operation.

Cons:

Complexity in Formation: Establishing an LLC could require more paperwork and legal processes than sole proprietorships or partnerships, perhaps needing expert help.

State-Specific rules: Operating an LLC entails conforming to state-specific rules, which may increase complexity and administrative difficulties.

Limited Fundraising Options: Compared to corporations, LLCs could encounter limits in collecting cash by issuing stocks or recruiting venture capital.

Self-Employment Taxes: In some cases, members of an LLC could be liable to self-employment taxes on their portion of the company's revenues

Potential Instability: The departure or death of a member may often generate dissolution or reorganization concerns inside the LLC.

Considering these characteristics is vital when determining if an LLC is the perfect fit for your company enterprise. While the advantages of limited liability and operational freedom are attractive, the administrative procedures and tax ramifications necessitate careful study before continuing with the establishment of an LLC.

1.3 Advantages and Disadvantages of Single and Multiple Member LLCs

Single-Member LLCs:

Advantages:

Simplified Management: Single-member LLCs provide simplified decision-making procedures since there's just one owner, leading to speedier and easier management.

Tax Flexibility: Taxation for single-member LLCs is generally straightforward, and frequently handled as a disregarded entity by the IRS, with earnings and losses recorded on the owner's tax return.

Personal Control: The owner maintains entire control over the business's operations, strategy, and decision-making without the requirement for agreement among various members.

Disadvantages:

Limited skills: With a single owner, there can be constraints in terms of various skills and viewpoints, thereby hurting the business's creativity and problem-solving ability.

Risk of Personal Liability: While single-member LLCs give liability protection, if the owner fails to maintain a clear division between personal and corporate money, there can be a risk of personal culpability.

Multiple-Member LLCs:

Advantages:

Diverse Skill Sets: Multiple-member LLCs benefit from a diversity of talents, expertise, and views brought in by diverse members, possibly increasing the business's decision-making and problem-solving abilities.

Shared obligations: With numerous owners, the load of decision-making and obligations is spread among members, allowing for collaborative management.

Risk Mitigation: Having several members may assist in minimizing risks and possible liabilities by distributing them among various persons.

Disadvantages:

Conflict Resolution: Disagreements among members could emerge, leading to possible conflicts in decision-making, management styles, or profit sharing, demanding explicit conflict resolution processes.

difficult Decision-Making: With several voices, decision-making could be more difficult, requiring consensus or formal voting methods, which might slow down the process.

Ultimately, the decision between a single-member and multiple-member LLC rests on the owner's tastes, company requirements, and long-term aspirations. While single-member LLCs provide simplicity and personal control, multiple-member LLCs give varied viewpoints but could entail more complicated management dynamics.

1.4 Should You Form an LLC?

Deciding whether to create an LLC relies on numerous criteria that cover your company objectives, risk tolerance, and operational necessities. Here are essential elements to assist you in assessing whether creating an LLC corresponds with your aspirations:

Liability Protection: If shielding personal assets from corporate obligations is a major consideration, incorporating an LLC might be useful. It divides your personal and corporate assets, insulating your riches from the debts and responsibilities of the firm.

Operational Flexibility: LLCs provide diversity in management structures and taxation alternatives, enabling you to adapt the company structure to meet your interests. If you desire freedom in operations and decision-making, an LLC can be an intriguing solution.

company Complexity: Consider the complexity of your company activities. If your firm entails major risks, assets, or dealings with the public, an LLC might offer a structured and protected framework.

Tax ramifications: Understanding the tax ramifications of an LLC is crucial. While LLCs frequently provide pass-through taxation, where earnings and losses are recorded on the owners' tax returns, it's vital to assess the tax advantages against possible complexity.

Long-Term Objectives: Reflect on your long-term company objectives. If you envisage development, recruiting investors, or ultimately going public, alternative company formats like corporations could be more suited, giving superior financing routes and governance frameworks.

Compliance and Administrative Requirements: Assess the administrative tasks and regulatory requirements connected with establishing an LLC. If you're okay with the paperwork and regulatory conformance, an LLC might be a beneficial alternative.

Costs and Resources: Consider the expenditures associated with creating and maintaining an LLC, including filing fees, legal aid, and continuing operating expenses. Evaluate if these prices correspond with your budget and resources.

In essence, incorporating an LLC may give a combination of liability protection, operational freedom, and streamlined taxes. However, the choice should be taken after a thorough review of your business's unique requirements and future objectives, and comprehending the legal and financial ramifications connected with an LLC form. Consulting legal and financial specialists may give crucial insights suited to your situation before making a final choice.

CHAPTER TWO

IS IT APPROPRIATE FOR YOUR ESTABLISHMENT?

2.1 Corporations Explored.

In researching the domain of company structures, it's vital to comprehend not only Limited Liability Companies (LLCs) but also other entities, notably corporations. Corporations constitute a different corporate structure apart from the people who control it.

Types of Corporations:

C Corporations (C-Corp): The most conventional form, allowing infinite development potential with the option to issue multiple classes of stock, recruiting investors, and even going public. C-Corps endure double taxation, where the firm pays taxes on income, and shareholders pay taxes on dividends received.

S Corporations (S-Corp): Unlike C-Corps, S-Corps enjoy pass-through taxes, eliminating double taxation. They are restricted to a maximum of 100 stockholders, all of whom must be U.S. citizens or residents, making them appropriate for smaller firms.

Distinct Features of Corporations:

Separate Legal Entity: Corporations operate separately from their owners, insulating people from personal culpability for corporate debts and responsibilities.

Shareholders and Board of Directors: Corporations have shareholders who own the firm and elect a board of directors responsible for strategic decisions and selecting officers to supervise daily operations.

Raising funds: Corporations have an edge in raising funds via issuing stocks or bonds, attracting investors, and aiding expansion.

Complexity and formality: Corporations include greater formality, such as frequent board meetings, tight record-keeping, and specialized reporting obligations, compared to other corporate forms.

Choosing Between LLCs and Corporations:

Deciding between an LLC and a corporation relies on numerous aspects, including your company goals, development ambitions, tax concerns, and management choices. Corporations are appropriate for bigger organizations seeking considerable expansion and access to financial markets but come with higher formality. Conversely, LLCs provide flexibility, streamlined administration, and pass-through taxes but could have restrictions in obtaining money and growth potential compared to corporations.

Understanding these characteristics is vital in making an educated choice regarding the most suited company structure for your entrepreneurial pursuits.

The Organizational Makeup of Corporations

The structure of companies is characterized by a hierarchical organization that describes the governance, decision-making, and operational framework. Here's an overview of the usual structure:

Shareholders: Shareholders are the proprietors of the company. They invest in the firm by acquiring shares of stock. Shareholders possess voting rights and influence the company's important decisions via their voting power at shareholder meetings.

Board of Directors: The board of directors is chosen by shareholders to supervise the corporation's administration and direction. They make strategic choices, hire senior executives (such as the CEO), and ensure that the company's operations fit with shareholders' interests.

Officers: Officers are responsible for the day-to-day operations and administration of the company. The major officials include the Chief Executive Officer (CEO), Chief Financial Officer (CFO), Chief Operating Officer (COO), and others, each handling specialized parts of the organization.

workers: Apart from the top officials, companies have workers who perform different duties and positions inside the organization. These personnel contribute to the day-to-day operations and the overall performance of the organization.

Key Points in the Structure:

Hierarchy: The organization functions under a defined hierarchy where the shareholders elect the board, the board controls the officers, and the officers manage the workforce.

responsibility: Each level of the system has a degree of responsibility. The board is responsible to the shareholders, executives are accountable to the board, and personnel are accountable to their managers.

Decision-Making Process: The decision-making process requires cooperation and monitoring at each level. Major decisions are normally taken by the board of directors, with input from officers based on their experience and operational insights.

Understanding the structure of organizations is vital as it specifies the roles, duties, and interactions among the major components. This structure helps preserve order, accountability, and efficient operations inside the company.

2.2 Different Types of LLCs

1. Member-Managed LLC:

In a Member-Managed LLC, all the owners, referred to as "members," actively engage in the company's daily operations and decision-making procedures. Each member owns a share in the firm and has a vote in its management. This form is prevalent among smaller or closely-held LLCs, particularly those with a limited number of owners who seek direct participation in operating the firm.

Key Characteristics:

Equal Participation: Each member has an equal voice in the company's activities, regardless of their investment or ownership share.

Direct Involvement: Members take an active involvement in the day-to-day operations, such as making business decisions, managing funds, and supervising corporate activities.

Flexibility: As members are directly engaged, choices may be taken quickly without the need for sophisticated voting or formal processes.

Communication and Consensus: Communication among members is key. While all members have decision-making capacity, consensus-building and open discourse play major roles in attaining cohesive actions.

Advantages:

Hands-On Management: Members have direct authority and engagement in the company, allowing for agility in decision-making and operations.

Unity and Shared Responsibility: Collaboration among members may generate a feeling of shared responsibility, dedication, and a single vision for the firm.

Considerations:

Potential for Disagreements: Differences in opinion among members might lead to disputes, underlining the necessity for efficient conflict resolution methods.

Dependency on Member Availability: Operations may be disrupted if one or more members are absent due to personal reasons, compromising the decision-making process or company continuity.

The Member-Managed LLC structure allows all owners to actively participate in the company, generating a feeling of ownership and participation. However, excellent communication, mutual respect, and shared objectives are important for the seamless functioning of this framework.

1. Manager-Managed LLC.

In a Manager-Managed LLC, the company's day-to-day operations and decision-making power are assigned to one or more designated managers instead of being directly managed by all the members. Let's go into the intricacies of this structure:

Manager-Managed LLC:

In this configuration, members designate one or more managers—either from among themselves or externally—to supervise the LLC's daily business. These managers perform operational chores, make strategic choices, and represent the organization in commercial interactions. The remaining members, referred known as "passive members," do not actively participate in the business's daily activities.

Key Characteristics:

Designated Managers: Individuals, whether members or paid professionals, take on management positions to oversee the company's operations.

Limited Active Involvement of Members: Members who are not managers have a more passive role, giving money, and sharing earnings, but are not actively engaged in the company's operations or decision-making.

Clear Division of Responsibilities: Managers are accountable for the day-to-day management, whereas non-manager members may have limited engagement until stipulated in the operating agreement.

Advantages:

experience in Management: Having appointed managers enables specialized experience to guide the company's activities.

Clear Decision-Making: Concentrated decision-making authority in managers simplifies operations and gives a clear hierarchy for implementing goals.

Considerations:

Dependence on management: The performance of the firm might greatly rely on the competence and judgments of the chosen management.

Potential Communication Gaps: If passive members feel separated from the decision-making process, communication and alignment could become problematic.

Use Case Scenarios:

Professional skills: Ideal for circumstances when members lack specialized skills or time to run day-to-day activities successfully.

Investor-Driven Ventures: Suited for instances where passive investors seek hands-off participation in operational concerns.

The Manager-Managed LLC form gives a clear division of labor, enabling specialist management while affording passive members the chance to participate without direct operational duties. Effective communication and a well-defined operating agreement are important to reconcile the duties of managers and passive members within this framework.

1. Domestic LLC:

State Registration: A Domestic LLC is founded and registered under the rules and regulations of the state in which it performs its major business activity.

Legal Recognition: It is recognized as a distinct legal entity from its owners, offering liability protection to its members within the state where it's registered.

Compliance: A Domestic LLC is required to comply with the state's requirements, including yearly filings, tax responsibilities, and adherence to state-specific rules regulating LLCs.

Key Attributes:

major Operations: A Domestic LLC performs its major business operations inside the state of its establishment.

State Laws and Regulations: It is subject to the laws, rules, and regulations of the state where it's registered, influencing taxes, reporting, and compliance duties.

Advantages:

Local Recognition: By operating inside a specified state, the LLC receives recognition and credibility within that jurisdiction.

Simplified Compliance: The LLC must comply with the rules and requirements of a single state, streamlining administrative procedures.

Considerations:

State-Specific Rules: Each state has its distinct legal and tax environment, affecting the LLC's activities and compliance.

Restrictions on activities: Some states may have prohibitions on doing business over state boundaries, perhaps requiring extra filings for activities in other states.

Use Case Scenarios:

Local enterprises: Suited for enterprises that principally operate and service clients inside a certain state.

Compliance Simplicity: Ideal for businesses seeking simplicity in conforming to a single state's legislation and standards.

Understanding the notion of a Domestic LLC is crucial for companies wishing to establish their legal presence inside a certain state, adhere to state-specific legislation, and benefit from the legal protection and recognition within that jurisdiction.

1. Foreign LLC.

A Foreign LLC is an LLC that has been incorporated in one state but operates or does business in another state where it wasn't initially founded. Here's a thorough overview:

Originating State: The Foreign LLC is initially founded and registered in a state, acting as its home jurisdiction.

Operations in Other States: When this LLC extends its operations or undertakes business activities beyond its home state, it's termed a Foreign LLC in those extra states.

Compliance: To operate in another state, a Foreign LLC must normally register with that state's authorities, completing particular criteria, such as obtaining a Certificate of Authority, paying fees, and complying with local legislation.

Key Attributes:

Multistate Operations: A Foreign LLC expands its commercial operations beyond its initial state of establishment into one or more additional states.

Compliance with Multiple States: It conforms with the rules, tax laws, and reporting requirements of both its home state and any states where it's registered as a Foreign LLC.

Advantages:

Extension Opportunities: Allows for the development and extension of company operations beyond state boundaries without having to incorporate a new LLC in each state.

Flexibility: Enables the LLC to access markets, resources, or possibilities in multiple states without founding new companies from the beginning.

Considerations:

Registration Requirements: Each state has its registration procedure, costs, and compliance duties for Foreign LLCs, which might vary greatly.

Complexity and expenditures: Registering as a Foreign LLC requires administrative complications, more paperwork, and continuing compliance expenditures in each state of operation.

Use Case Scenarios:

Business Expansion: Suited for enterprises wanting to grow their operations and presence across many states without founding new corporations.

Regional or nationwide Ventures: Ideal for enterprises wishing to operate on a regional or nationwide scale without the limits of a single state's borders.

Understanding the notion of a Foreign LLC is vital for firms wishing to expand their activities outside their initial place of creation, allowing for growth while conforming to the legal and regulatory requirements of numerous countries.

1. Professional Limited Liability Company.

A Professional Limited Liability Company (PLLC) is a specialized kind of LLC typically founded for licensed professionals, such as physicians, attorneys, architects, accountants, and other professional service providers. Let's investigate its specifics:

Specific to Licensed Experts: PLLCs are customized for firms offering professional services when state law dictates that these experts establish their company as an LLC rather than a regular partnership or corporation.

Liability Protection: Similar to an LLC, a PLLC offers limited liability protection to its members (licensed professionals) from business debts and legal proceedings originating from the activities of other members, employees, or the firm itself.

State Licensing Requirements: To organize a PLLC, members often need to have particular professional licenses needed by the state where the PLLC is founded.

Key Characteristics:

Professional Services: The PLLC structure is particularly created for organizations supplying professional services, assuring compliance with state licensing standards.

Limited responsibility: Members are typically insulated from personal responsibility stemming from the conduct or malpractice of other members within the PLLC.

Advantages:

Liability Protection: Offers limited liability protection to individual members against the conduct or malpractice of other members within the PLLC.

Professional Compliance: Complies with state requirements demanding licensed professionals to incorporate their enterprises as PLLCs for liability protection.

Considerations:

Licensing Requirements: Members must possess valid professional licenses in the state where the PLLC operates, and there can be limits on the sorts of professionals who can create a PLLC.

State-Specific Regulations: Requirements for creating a PLLC, including licensing and continuing compliance, differ by state.

Use Case Scenarios:

Professional Services: Suitable for organizations when licensed professionals supply services needing liability protection yet are compelled to operate within the constraints of a PLLC structure.

Risk Management: Ideal for professionals wishing to shield personal assets against business-related liabilities and possible malpractice claims.

Understanding the notion of a PLLC is vital for licensed professionals wishing to establish their company companies in line with state legislation, assuring both liability protection and the practice of their professions within the boundaries of legal frameworks.

1. Series Limited Liability Company

A Series Limited Liability Company (Series LLC) is a unique legal structure that allows for the development of distinct "series" inside a single LLC, each having its assets, liabilities, and members. Let's go more into its specifics:

Distinct Segments: Within a Series LLC, each series behaves as an independent entity, shielding its assets and liabilities from other series within the same LLC.

Independence: Each series may have its own corporate goals, assets, members, and obligations, offering a degree of separation equivalent to independent organizations under one roof.

Operational Flexibility: Allows for numerous business operations or investments to be compartmentalized inside one LLC structure, minimizing administrative overhead compared to operating separate businesses.

Key Characteristics:

Segmented Structure: It works as a single legal body with the capacity to construct different series, each having its rights, objectives, and liabilities.

Asset Protection: The obligation of each series is normally restricted to that specific series, giving a degree of insulation between the assets and liabilities of various series.

Advantages:

Risk Segmentation: Allows for the separation of risks connected with distinct company operations, insulating assets in one series from liabilities incurred in another.

Cost Efficiency: Eliminates the need to organize several LLCs for various company operations, saving administrative and registration expenses.

Considerations:

State Regulations: Not all states recognize Series LLCs and those that do could have differing laws on their establishment and operation.

Legal Complexity: Operating a Series LLC needs thorough record-keeping and compliance to maintain an unambiguous distinction between series.

Use Case Scenarios:

Real Estate Investments: Suitable for real estate investors wishing to segregate assets and liabilities of numerous properties under one umbrella business.

Venture Capital: Ideal for managing various investment portfolios or venture capital operations, allowing for segregation and administration of each investment within discrete series.

Understanding the Series LLC structure is vital for organizations seeking a flexible and efficient approach to compartmentalize risks, manage several projects, or separate assets and liabilities under a single legal entity while conforming to state-specific legislation and compliance requirements.

2.3 What to Consider When Choosing a Type of LLC

1. Number of Members.

When determining the form of LLC that meets your requirements, various aspects come into play. Here, we'll start by analyzing the relevance of the number of members participating in the LLC:

Single-Member LLC: This form of LLC has one owner, allowing ease in decision-making and administration, yet the owner retains complete control and undertakes all obligations and liabilities.

Multiple-Member LLC: Involves more than one owner, spreading duties, decision-making, and capital contributions among members. It may boost resources and views but could hinder decision-making owing to various viewpoints.

Key Points to Consider:

Ownership Dynamics: Decide whether the LLC will have a single owner or several members to correspond with your company goal and governance structure.

Decision-Making Process: Evaluate how the number of members could affect the decision-making process within the LLC and examine the consequences for operations and growth.

Advantages:

Single-Member LLC: Provides simplicity, ease of decision-making, and direct control for the one owner.

Multiple-Member LLC: Allows for different viewpoints, shared tasks, and possibly enhanced resources and experience.

Considerations:

Agreement and Consensus: Multiple-member LLCs can need specific agreements and norms to govern decision-making and any disputes among members.

Complexity vs. Control: Single-member LLCs give clear control, whereas multiple-member LLCs provide variety but could add complexity to operations and decision-making.

Use Case Scenarios:

Single-Member LLC: Ideal for solitary entrepreneurs wanting autonomy, control, and simplicity in conducting their company operations.

many-Member LLC: Suited for enterprises with partners or many stakeholders looking to harness varied skill sets, resources, and views to drive the company's development and operations.

The number of members of an LLC greatly determines its dynamics, decision-making processes, and governance structure. Understanding these ramifications is vital when deciding the most appropriate form of LLC for your company's objectives and operational requirements.

1. Everyday Functions of Members.

The duties carried out by members within an LLC play a crucial role in its operation and profitability. Let's study the relevance of these routine functions:

Management responsibilities: Members of an LLC often take on different responsibilities, such as managers or passive investors, deciding their participation in the day-to-day activities.

Decision-Making: Active members could engage in crucial decisions, strategic planning, and managing corporate operations, while passive members might have limited participation in business activities.

Key Points to Consider:

Active vs. Passive Roles: Determine the level of engagement members will have in managing the LLC's operations in line with their knowledge, availability, and commitment.

Defined obligations: Clarify the tasks and obligations of each member to eliminate uncertainty and guarantee a smooth operation of the LLC.

Advantages:

Diverse Skill Sets: Active people giving their skills and engagement may increase decision-making and operational efficiency.

Flexibility: Passive members may profit from investment returns without the necessity for active engagement in day-to-day activities.

Considerations:

Clarity in duties: Identifying the duties and obligations of each member may reduce disputes and misunderstandings.

Decision-Making Framework: An organized decision-making process guarantees efficient operations and avoids delays or disagreements.

Use Case Scenarios:

Active Participation: Members actively participate in the LLC, managing operations, making strategic choices, and offering knowledge to foster development and success.

Passive Investment: Members want investment returns but choose minimal participation in everyday operations, leaving others to handle management and decision-making.

Understanding the daily activities and roles of members within an LLC is vital for creating clear expectations, clarifying responsibilities, and promoting successful cooperation among members to accomplish the business's objectives.

1. Should you Register Your LLC as Domestic or Foreign?

When forming an LLC, selecting whether to register it as a domestic or international company depends on where the firm operates and where it was first founded.

Domestic vs. Foreign LLC:

Domestic LLC: This refers to an LLC registered in the state where it was founded and performs its major business activities.

Foreign LLC: Contrary to its name, a foreign LLC doesn't always indicate it's based worldwide. It signifies an LLC that's registered in one state but does business in another state.

Factors to Consider:

Primary Place of Business: If your LLC operates and conducts the bulk of its business in the state where it's created, it's normally registered as a domestic LLC.

Expansion and Operations: If your LLC extends operations into a state different from where it was created, it may need to register as a foreign LLC in that state to lawfully do business there.

Advantages:

Compliance: Registering your LLC correctly assures compliance with state laws, tax rules, and other legal obligations in the states where your firm operates.

Legal Clarity: Proper registration helps preserve legal standing, streamlines transactions, and gives clarity on taxes and liability problems.

Considerations:

State-Specific Requirements: Each state has its requirements concerning international LLCs, including registration costs, taxes, and reporting duties.

Timing of Registration: Timely registration as a foreign LLC is vital before initiating operations in a new state to prevent any fines or legal complications.

Use Case Scenarios:

Local Operations: A company mainly operating and located in one state often registers as a domestic LLC in that state.

Expansion: When extending operations into additional states, registering as a foreign LLC in those jurisdictions assures compliance with local legislation and legal standing.

Deciding whether to register your LLC as a domestic or international company relies on where your firm operates and performs its core operations. Understanding the differences helps maintain compliance with state legislation and allows seamless operations across numerous sites.

1. Are the Members Licensed Professionals?

Determining whether members of an LLC need to be licensed professionals relies on the nature of the firm and the particular rules imposed by the state or industry.

Licensed Professionals in an LLC:

Regulated Professions: Certain sectors or professions, such as law, medicine, accountancy, real estate, and others, require those working within them to obtain specialized professional licenses.

State Regulations: Some states specify that particular companies or services may only be delivered by persons possessing proper professional licenses.

Key Considerations:

Industry Requirements: Assess if the industry or services supplied by the LLC demand members to possess professional licenses.

Legal Compliance: Ensure compliance with state rules governing licensed professionals and their role inside the LLC.

Advantages:

Credibility and Trust: Having licensed experts inside the LLC may promote credibility and trust among clients and consumers, displaying knowledge and adherence to professional norms.

Legal Compliance: It assures conformity to state rules, avoiding possible legal challenges or fines associated with unauthorized practice.

Considerations:

Licensing Obligations: Determine if the nature of the company needs licensed experts to maintain compliance with industry standards and regulatory obligations.

Liability and supervision: Understand the liabilities and obligations connected with licensed professions inside the LLC and the supervision they could necessitate.

Use Case Scenarios:

Legal and Medical Services: Businesses offering legal or medical services often need licensed professionals within their ownership or operating structure.

Specialized Industries: Professions like accountancy, engineering, architecture, or real estate could need licensed experts in an LLC to deliver unique services.

Determining whether LLC members need to be licensed professionals includes knowing industry-specific legislation and state standards. Ensuring compliance with these standards is vital to prevent legal issues and preserve reputation within the particular sector of activity.

1. Is the Point of the LLC to Create Multiple Opportunities?

Determining whether the aim of founding an LLC is to offer various possibilities includes assessing the fundamental goals and objectives behind establishing the company structure.

Exploring the Purpose of the LLC:

Business Objectives: Consider if the LLC was mainly founded to grab diverse business possibilities, diversify operations, or pursue many projects concurrently.

Expansion and Growth: Assess if the LLC plans to grow into other markets, industries, or sectors to capitalize on varied commercial chances.

Key Considerations:

Strategic Goals: Understand whether the LLC's establishment matches with a plan to investigate and capitalize on many business possibilities concurrently.

Diversification: Evaluate if the LLC wants to diversify its activities, services, or goods to tap into multiple market sectors.

Advantages:

Versatility: Creating an LLC to explore several options might give flexibility in exploring different company operations, thereby boosting profits.

Risk Mitigation: Diversification among multiple prospects within an LLC might minimize the total risk associated with depending on a single business route.

Considerations:

Resource Allocation: Pursuing several possibilities could demand large resources, including funds, time, and personnel.

Management issues: Managing numerous endeavors concurrently might bring issues in resource allocation, decision-making, and operational management.

Use Case Scenarios:

Venture Capital or Holding Companies: Entities generally created to invest in or maintain ownership across many enterprises, aiming for diverse investment portfolios.

Entrepreneurial Ventures: Some entrepreneurs incorporate LLCs to investigate and develop many company concepts or companies simultaneously.

Determining if an LLC is meant to provide many possibilities entails analyzing its strategic goals, diversification aims, and preparedness to handle several businesses concurrently. It's necessary to assess the benefits against the possible obstacles connected with pursuing several possibilities inside the LLC structure.

CHAPTER THREE

STARTING AN LLC.

3.1 The Seven Steps.

1. Step One: Choosing a Name

Selecting an acceptable name for your Limited Liability Company (LLC) signifies the fundamental step in creating your company structure. This approach covers numerous essential factors to maintain legal compliance and brand identity.

Uniqueness: Ensure the name you pick is unique and not currently in use by another firm in your state. This eliminates legal issues and misunderstandings in the market.

Legal Requirements: Comply with your state's LLC naming rules. Often, the name must include certain terms like "Limited Liability Company" or its acronyms (e.g., LLC, L.L.C.).

Avoid Restricted Terms: Some terms—like "bank," "insurance," or "university"—require extra paperwork or permits if used in an LLC name, ensuring the name corresponds with your company activity.

Trademark Checks: Conduct a thorough check to confirm your selected name isn't already trademarked. This measure defends your company from future legal challenges.

Reflect Brand Identity: Choose a name that connects with your brand's goal, objectives, and values. A fascinating name may add to brand awareness and market placement.

Points to Consider During the Name Selection Process:

Creativity and Memorability: Aim for a name that's simple to remember and stands out in your sector or market.

Domain Availability: Consider the availability of a related domain name for your company website.

Future Growth: Choose a name that supports possible corporate growth or diversification.

Check State Databases: Verify the name's availability by searching the state's business name database.

Next Steps after Name Selection:

Once you've agreed on a name:

Confirm its availability: Check with your state's business name database.

Reserve the name: Some jurisdictions enable name reserve for a specified time to safeguard it while finishing the formation procedure.

Register the name: When submitting Articles of Organization, your selected name will be formally registered with the state.

Careful study and respect for legal and branding guidelines throughout the name-choosing stage build a strong basis for your LLC, impacting its market presence and legal compliance from the beginning.

1. Step Two: Appointing a Registered Agent.

Appointing a registered agent is a critical stage in the creation of an LLC, assuring legal compliance and efficient communication between your firm and the state.

Understanding the Role of a Registered Agent:

Legal Liaison: A registered agent acts as the official point of contact between the LLC and the state government, receiving legal and official papers on behalf of the firm.

Legal Requirement: Most states demand that LLCs choose a registered agent with a physical address inside the state where the LLC is registered.

Qualities of a Registered Agent:

Physical Address: The agent must have a physical street address within the state of formation where legal papers may be reliably received during business hours.

Availability: The agent must be accessible during regular business hours to receive legal papers and official notifications.

Legal and commercial Knowledge: Understanding of legal and commercial concerns assists in organizing and transmitting crucial papers swiftly.

Options for a Registered Agent:

Individuals: You, a business partner, or any other person linked with the LLC may act as the registered agent provided they match the qualifications.

Professional Registered Agent Services: Utilizing professional registered agent services may assure compliance and effective management of legal paperwork. These services frequently give a physical location and are accessible during business hours.

Responsibilities of the Registered Agent:

Receiving Legal papers: They receive legal notifications, official communications, and service of process (legal papers linked to litigation) on behalf of the LLC.

Forwarding papers: Once received, the agent transmits these papers quickly to the LLC's authorized contact.

Benefits of a Professional Registered Agent Service:

Compliance Assurance: Professional services assure compliance with state rules regulating registered agents.

Privacy and Convenience: Using a service may ensure privacy by keeping personal addresses off public records, and it gives convenience as they handle the administrative procedures associated with legal paperwork.

Selecting a person or a professional business as your registered agent is a key choice, ensuring your LLC satisfies its legal requirements and works efficiently by receiving and maintaining important legal papers. Consider the agent's availability, dependability, and expertise in legal concerns while making this decision.

1. Step Three: Obtaining the Articles of Organization Form.

Acquiring the Articles of Organization form is a vital step in the process of creating your Limited Liability Company (LLC). This document, also known as a Certificate of Formation in certain jurisdictions, is the fundamental documentation necessary by the state to formally register your LLC.

Key Aspects of the Articles of Organization:

Information Requirement: The form normally seeks basic facts about your LLC, such as the firm name, primary address, registered agent details, and occasionally, the purpose of the LLC.

Legal Document: It's a legal document submitted with the Secretary of State or appropriate state office, commencing the incorporation of your LLC.

Filing price: There is normally a price involved with filing the Articles of Organization, which varies by state.

Steps Involved in Obtaining the Articles of Organization:

State criteria: Understand your state's particular criteria for the Articles of Organization. These may change greatly from state to state.

Form Access: Obtain the form from the Secretary of State's website or the appropriate state office responsible for company registrations. Some states permit online submission, while others require mail or in-person filing.

Completion of the Form: Fill out the form correctly, supplying all necessary information. Ensure conformity with the state's name traditions and regulatory criteria for LLC establishment.

Filing and Submission: Pay the relevant filing fee and send the completed form to the appropriate state office within the jurisdiction where you wish to run your LLC.

Contents of the Articles of Organization Form:

LLC Name: Clearly explain the selected company name as per state standards.

Registered Agent Information: Provide information about the designated registered agent, including their physical location inside the state.

Business Address: Mention the major office address of the LLC.

length of the LLC (if applicable): Some states require defining the LLC's planned length, particularly if it's not permanent.

Management Structure: Some states may inquire about the LLC's management structure, distinguishing whether it's member-managed or manager-managed.

After Submission:

Confirmation and Processing: Once filed, the state will process the Articles of Organization. Upon approval, you'll get a stamped or certified copy as evidence of your LLC's existence.

Obtaining and accurately completing the Articles of Organization is a vital basic step in forming an LLC. Ensuring accuracy and compliance with state legislation is crucial to starting the official legal registration of your company organization.

1. Step Four: Preparing the Articles of Association Form

In many states, the Articles of Organization (sometimes called the Certificate of Formation) mainly create the LLC, while the Operating Agreement oversees its internal activities. The Articles of Organization generally concentrate on fundamental corporate information needed by the state, while the Operating Agreement is an internal document that specifies how the LLC will be operated.

The agreement comparable to the Articles of Association is commonly referred to as the Operating Agreement. This agreement is a vital internal document that specifies the operational and financial choices and structures of the LLC.

Key Aspects of the Operating Agreement:

Internal Governance: It specifies how the LLC will be administered, controlled, and structured, including numerous features such as member positions, voting rights, decision-making processes, profit distribution, and management procedures.

adjustable: The Operating Agreement is extremely adjustable and enables the members to modify the rules and regulations to match the unique requirements and conditions of the LLC.

Legal Requirement: Although not necessarily obligatory in every state, having an Operating Agreement is generally advised, as it helps minimize misunderstandings and disagreements among members in the future.

Contents of an Operating Agreement:

Member Roles and Obligations: Define the roles and obligations of each member inside the LLC.

Decision-Making Processes: Outline the process for making company choices, voting rights, and processes for resolving disagreements.

Capital Contributions and Profits: Detail the contributions made by each member, profit-sharing agreements, and how money will be allocated.

Management Structure: Specify whether the LLC will be administered by its members or by designated management.

Drafting the Operating Agreement:

Customization: Consider the particular objectives, aims, and structure of the LLC while establishing the Operating Agreement.

Legal aid: While templates are accessible, getting legal counsel or hiring professional aid may guarantee the agreement conforms with state laws and responds to the particular requirements of the firm.

Unanimous assent: Ensure that all members examine and assent to the provisions contained in the Operating Agreement before completing it.

Document Maintenance: Keep the Operating Agreement current and available to all members. Regular review and possible revisions may accommodate changes in the company or membership.

Conclusion:

The Articles of Organization create the LLC legally with the state, while the Operating Agreement oversees its internal activities. Crafting a detailed Operating Agreement customized to the LLC's requirements is a vital step toward defining clear standards and guaranteeing smooth operations inside the organization.

1. Step Five: Filing the Articles of Association Form

The stage of submitting the Articles of Association or Operating Agreement differs based on the terminology used and the particular regulations imposed by the state in which you're creating your LLC. Generally, after completing the Operating Agreement, the following procedure entails submitting it to the proper state agency or authority.

Filing the Operating Agreement:

State Guidelines: Check the particular requirements of your state about the filing procedure for the Operating Agreement or equivalent papers. Some states don't need the filing of the Operating Agreement as part of the LLC establishment procedure.

Submission Methods: Determine if your state requires the Operating Agreement to be submitted with the Articles of Organization during the LLC creation procedure or whether it has to be filed separately.

Filing expenses: Be aware of any related expenses for filing the Operating Agreement, if required by your state.

Submission Channels: Some jurisdictions enable online submission, while others may involve sending or submitting the paperwork in person to the Secretary of State or designated corporate entity agency.

Key Considerations:

Compliance: Ensure that the Operating Agreement conforms with your state's legal requirements for LLCs.

Legal Clarity: Draft the Operating Agreement using clear and unambiguous wording to eliminate any misunderstandings or disagreements among LLC members.

Legal Assistance: Consider getting legal counsel or professional guidance to evaluate the Operating Agreement, ensuring it fulfills legal criteria and appropriately reflects the LLC's interests.

After Submission:

Confirmation of Receipt: Once submitted, the state agency will process the document. You'll get confirmation of the filing, which can include a stamped or certified copy returned to you as proof of submission.

Ongoing Maintenance: Keep a copy of the filed Operating Agreement and preserve it among your LLC's official papers. Periodically evaluate and revise the agreement as appropriate, particularly in reaction to changes within the company or membership structure.

Filing the Operating Agreement or comparable document with the state is a vital step in defining the internal governance and operational parameters of your LLC. It formalizes the structure and operation of the firm as stated by the members, giving a blueprint for successful management and decision-making processes inside the organization.

1. Step Six: The Operating Agreement

The Operating Agreement is a crucial agreement that delineates the internal workings and governance structure of an LLC. It functions as a template for how the business will run, specifying rights, obligations, and decision-making processes among its members.

Key Components of the Operating Agreement:

Member Responsibilities and Responsibilities: Define the responsibilities and obligations of each member inside the LLC. This section describes their rights, voting abilities, and contributions to the corporation.

administration Structure: Clarify whether the LLC will be governed by its members (member-managed) or whether the administration will be entrusted to chosen managers (manager-managed).

Decision-Making Processes: Detail the decision-making methods, voting rules, and how significant firm choices will be decided.

Profit Distribution: Specify how earnings and losses will be divided among members and if payouts will be based on ownership percentages or other factors.

Capital Contributions: Outline the initial contributions made by each member to create the LLC, as well as processes for subsequent capital contributions as necessary.

Rules for Admission and Departure of Members: Include rules explaining how new members may join the LLC and the procedure for members quitting the firm or transferring their interests.

Dispute Resolution: Include means for resolving disagreements among members, such as mediation or arbitration processes, to lessen possible conflicts.

Drafting the Operating Agreement:

Customization: Tailor the agreement to meet the particular goals, aims, and circumstances of the LLC and its members.

Legal Compliance: Ensure compliance with state laws and regulations regulating LLCs. Consider getting legal assistance to ensure conformity to relevant legislation.

Unanimous Consent: Obtain unanimous agreement among all members before signing the Operating Agreement to avoid future disputes or misunderstandings.

Regular examination and Amendments: Periodically examine the Operating Agreement and revise it as appropriate to reflect any changes inside the LLC or among its members.

Significance of the Operating Agreement:

Internal Governance: Serves as a fundamental document defining the internal rules and processes for administering the LLC.

Dispute Prevention: Helps in preventing arguments among members by creating clear criteria for decision-making and conflict resolution.

Legal and company Clarity: Establishes a clear framework for managing the company, and protects the interests of the LLC and its members.

Crafting a complete Operating Agreement is vital for promoting smooth operations, defining standards for decision-making, and building a structure for the company's governance. It works as a fundamental document directing the business's development and relationships among its members.

1. Step Seven: Keep Your LLC Alive

Keeping an LLC active and complying with legal and regulatory standards is vital for its prolonged existence and good standing. This continuing role entails numerous critical acts to assure the LLC's continuation and adherence to different requirements.

Maintaining Your LLC's Active Status:

Regular Compliance: Fulfill all continuing state obligations, such as submitting yearly reports, paying state fees, and renewing licenses or permits, to keep the LLC's current existence.

Compliance with Operating Agreement: Continuously adhere to the parameters established in the Operating Agreement, ensuring that the LLC's activities correspond with the agreed-upon internal governance structure.

Tax duties: Comply with federal, state, and local tax requirements by filing relevant tax returns, making timely payments, and performing any tax-related duties particular to the LLC structure.

Record-Keeping: Maintain accurate and current records, including financial statements, meeting minutes, and any revisions made to the Operating Agreement, guaranteeing compliance and transparency.

yearly Meetings: Conduct and record yearly meetings, if required by the Operating Agreement or state legislation, to address critical business topics and decisions.

Registered Agent: Ensure the LLC maintains a registered agent in the state of creation or operation to receive legal and official correspondence on behalf of the business.

Amendments and Updates: Periodically review and revise the Operating Agreement as required to reflect changes in the LLC's structure, membership, or operating practices.

Avoiding Default: Avoid defaulting on state obligations, such as non-payment of fees or failing to submit appropriate paperwork, to avert possible fines or loss of good standing.

Consequences of Non-Compliance:

Administrative Dissolution: Failure to fulfill state compliance standards might result in the administrative dissolution of the LLC, resulting in loss of legal protections and liability shielding.

fines and Fees: Non-compliance may result in monetary fines, late fees, or legal implications, harming the LLC's financial stability and reputation.

responsibility Exposure: Loss of LLC registration due to non-compliance could subject members to personal responsibility for company debts and obligations.

Conclusion:

Maintaining the active status of an LLC needs continuing dedication and adherence to legal, financial, and operational duties. By maintaining compliance with state legislation, satisfying tax obligations, and respecting the provisions specified in the Operating Agreement, the LLC may guarantee its continuation and legal standing in doing business. Regular monitoring, record-keeping, and timely actions are necessary to keep the LLC working efficiently and in good standing.

3.2 Business Credit

Establishing and maintaining company credit is vital for an LLC's financial health and development. Building a high credit rating allows the organization to acquire financing, get advantageous terms from suppliers, and exhibit financial trustworthiness. Here's an outline of managing business credit for your LLC:

Understanding Business Credit:

Separation of Personal and Company Credit: As an LLC, maintain a clear difference between personal and company funds to develop a unique corporate credit profile.

trustworthiness: Build trustworthiness by creating accounts in the LLC's name, such as a company bank account, acquiring a federal employment identification number (EIN), and applying for a D-U-N-S number from Dun & Bradstreet.

Building Business Credit:

Open Vendor Accounts: Establish credit with suppliers that submit payment history to credit agencies, eventually developing a favorable credit history for the LLC.

Business Credit Cards: Apply for a business credit card in the LLC's name and use it wisely to establish credit.

Small Business Loans: Seek small business loans or lines of credit, ensuring regular repayments to establish trustworthiness.

Managing Business Credit:

Timely Payments: Pay invoices and credit obligations on time, since late payments adversely damage the LLC's credit score.

Credit usage: Maintain a low credit usage ratio by utilizing just a percentage of available credit, since excessive use might damage credit ratings.

Regular Monitoring: Regularly analyze credit reports from major business credit agencies including Dun & Bradstreet, Experian, and Equifax to check for mistakes or fraud.

Benefits of Good Business Credit:

Access to finance: Establishing excellent credit allows easier access to finance choices, including loans and lines of credit, for company development and expansion.

Favorable Terms: A great credit profile may lead to better terms from suppliers, cheaper interest rates on loans, and bigger credit limits.

Business Credibility: A solid credit history boosts the LLC's reputation and credibility in the eyes of lenders, suppliers, and future business partners.

Conclusion:

Managing and growing company credit is a vital component of assuring financial stability and success for your LLC. By opening credit accounts, keeping regular payments, and monitoring credit reports, the LLC may create a positive credit profile, unlocking prospects for financing and increasing its overall financial health.

3.3 Which State(s) to File Your Operating Agreement in

1. Filing in Your Home State

Filing the Operating Agreement in your home state provides various benefits and conforms with normal LLC procedures. Here's a full take on the pros and considerations of filing your Operating Agreement in your home state:

Advantages of Filing in Your Home State:

Legal conformity: Filing in your home state assures conformity with local legislation since each state has its own set of rules and standards regulating LLCs.

Convenience: Operating in your home state streamlines administrative chores, such as yearly filings, tax requirements, and compliance with state rules, making it more straightforward to handle the LLC's business.

Physical Presence: If your firm works mostly inside your home state, filing the Operating Agreement there coincides with your business's physical presence, proving a concrete link to the state.

Local Laws and Courts: Operating inside your home state means you'll be subject to the local legal system and courts, which may give familiarity and convenience in case of legal issues or processes.

Business Relations: Filing in your home state may establish better ties with local suppliers, consumers, and stakeholders who prefer dealing with firms registered inside the same state.

Considerations for Filing in Your Home State:

State-Specific Requirements: Different states have varied filing costs, yearly report requirements, and rules. Understanding these state-specific duties is vital before submitting.

Foreign Qualification: If your LLC operates in several jurisdictions, you may need to qualify as a foreign LLC in those states, even if the Operating Agreement is filed in your home state.

Legal Advice: Seeking legal advice or a professional adviser may give insights into state-specific needs, assuring compliance and knowing any peculiarities in your own state's rules.

Filing your Operating Agreement in your home state is frequently the default and preferred alternative, particularly if your firm predominantly operates inside that state. It corresponds with local legislation, streamlines administrative procedures, and displays a strong relationship between the firm and its home state. However, establish a full grasp of your state's rules and consider getting expert help to handle any complications.

1. Filing in a Foreign State.

Filing your Operating Agreement in a foreign state, also known as foreign qualifying, happens when your LLC is created or registered in a state other than your principal place of business. Here's an overview of the concerns and advantages of registering your Operating Agreement in a foreign state:

Considerations for Filing in a Foreign State:

Business Expansion: If your LLC expects to operate and conduct substantial business in a state other than your home state, international qualification could be essential to lawfully operate there.

Multi-State Operations: If your LLC does business in many states, particularly when there's a physical presence or large transactions in another state, international qualification could be necessary by law.

Compliance Requirements: Each state has its own set of requirements governing international LLCs. This involves extra paperwork, costs, and compliance duties such as yearly reports or taxes in the foreign state.

Legal safeguards: Filing in a foreign state gives legal protection in that state, enabling the LLC to do business while benefitting from certain legal safeguards and access to that state's courts.

Benefits of Filing in a Foreign State:

Access to Markets: Qualifying as a foreign LLC in a different state improves market access, enabling the firm to lawfully operate and create a presence in various areas.

Legal Protection: Foreign qualification gives legal validity and protection in the foreign state, assuring the LLC's conformity with local laws and regulations.

company Flexibility: Operating in several states via international qualification enables company flexibility by permitting growth and tapping into new markets.

Considerations and Challenges:

Increased Complexity: Managing compliance standards, taxes, and administrative duties in many states may be complicated and may need more administrative time and resources.

Additional expenditures: Filing fees, yearly report fees, and compliance expenditures in each state may raise the LLC's operational expenses.

Legal Advice: Consulting legal specialists or consultants knowledgeable about the individual state's regulations is vital to guarantee correct compliance and awareness of the ramifications of foreign certification.

Deciding to register your Operating Agreement in a foreign state should be a strategic choice based on your business's development ambitions, operational demands, and legal requirements. It's necessary to assess the advantages against the complications and expenses involved in maintaining compliance across various states. Consulting legal counsel may give helpful advice in making this choice.

3.4 States That Are Disadvantageous to Register Your LLC

Determining which states can be unfavorable for creating your LLC relies on several criteria, including taxes, fees, laws, and legal issues. Here are elements to consider when analyzing states that can be less favorable for registering your LLC:

High Tax States:

1. High Tax Rates: States with high-income taxes, corporation taxes, or franchise taxes could cause financial problems for LLCs, particularly those with large revenue or profits.

Complex Regulatory Environments:

2. rigorous rules: States with complicated or rigorous rules may impose significant compliance costs, administrative procedures, or licensing duties on LLCs.

Legal Limitations:

3. Legal Restrictions: Some states could have restrictive business regulations, banning particular kinds of industries or corporate structures, which might be unfavorable for specific LLC types or activities.

Unfavorable Business Environment:

4. High Operating expenses: States with high operating expenses, like rent, labor, or utilities, could impair the overall profitability and feasibility of an LLC.

Specific Examples:

5. State-Specific Challenges: Certain states are commonly described as tough for business owing to variables like high taxes (e.g., California), complicated regulatory regimes (e.g., New York), or costly living and operations expenditures (e.g., Hawaii).

Considerations for Disadvantageous States:

Financial effect: Assess the effect of taxes, fees, and compliance expenditures on your LLC's bottom line.

Regulatory Burden: Evaluate the ease of conducting business based on the state's regulatory requirements.

sector Relevance: Consider whether the state has constraints or rules that could directly affect your unique sector or company strategy.

Mitigation Strategies:

Registered Agent Services: Engage registered agent services that may assist in negotiating state-specific compliance requirements.

Professional assistance: Seek legal or financial assistance to comprehend the ramifications and design methods to address any issues in adverse states.

It's crucial to undertake comprehensive research and evaluate the particular demands of your LLC while choosing states for registration. What can be detrimental for one LLC might not necessarily apply to another. Carefully analyzing these variables will assist in making an educated choice when picking the most suited state for your LLC's registration.

3.5 Do I Need a Lawyer to Register My LLC?

While it's not required to engage a lawyer to form an LLC, receiving legal counsel may be useful, particularly when dealing with complicated legal requirements. Here are issues surrounding the requirement of a lawyer for LLC registration:

Self-Registration:

DIY Approach: Many businesses successfully register their LLCs independently by following state-specific rules accessible online. This strategy can save expenditures.

Complexities and Legal Guidance:

2. Legal Nuances: If your LLC structure or activities contain complications like many members, special agreements, or particular industry requirements, legal guidance assures correct compliance.

Ensuring Accuracy:

3. Correct Documentation: Lawyers assist in ensuring the correct completion of relevant documentation, decreasing the possibility of mistakes or omissions that can lead to issues.

Addressing Legal Concerns:

4. Legal Protection: Lawyers may assist in liability protection, member agreements, tax ramifications, and other legal factors that can influence the LLC's form and activities.

Cost-Benefit Analysis:

5. expense Consideration: Balancing the expense of legal services against the possible rewards and dangers involved in ensuring appropriate registration and compliance is vital.

When to Consider Legal Counsel:

Complex Situations: If your LLC structure or activities are sophisticated or include particular legal constraints.

Risk Mitigation: To limit legal risks, particularly when dealing with possible liability concerns or industry-specific rules.

Customized Agreements: Drafting customized operational agreements or contracts among members could need legal competence.

Alternative Options:

Online Services: Online platforms provide economical services that help people through the LLC formation procedure.

Consultation: Even if not engaging a lawyer for the full procedure, a consultation session with a legal professional may give insights and direction for a simpler registration.

While it's not obligatory, contacting or employing a lawyer for LLC registration is suggested in scenarios requiring complexity, unusual circumstances, or where legal assistance might preserve the LLC's interests. Assess your requirements, the intricacy of your company, and possible legal ramifications before deciding on whether to employ legal advice for LLC registration.

CHAPTER FOUR

COMMON MISTAKES WHEN STARTING AN LLC.

4.1 Six Very Common Mistakes.

1. Choosing the Wrong Entity

Choosing the improper entity form for your LLC is a major error that may have lasting effects. Common problems in entity selection include:

Failure to Understand Entity Types: Not knowing the distinctions between different company forms (including LLCs, corporations, and partnerships) and their ramifications on responsibility, taxes, and administration.

Ignoring Future Development Plans: Selecting an entity structure without considering future business development could lead to constraints or complexity as the organization develops.

Tax Implications Oversight: Overlooking the tax repercussions associated with various entity forms results in unanticipated tax obligations or inefficiencies.

Disregarding Liability Protection: Opting for a corporate structure that doesn't give enough liability protection, thereby exposing personal assets to business-related liabilities.

Inadequate Flexibility: Choosing a structure that lacks the flexibility required for the LLC's operating and managerial needs.

Ignoring state-specific legislation: failing to investigate and grasp state-specific legislation and requirements linked to different entity kinds results in non-compliance difficulties.

Selecting the suitable entity type for your LLC is basic and involves comprehensive study, knowledge, and consideration of long-term company objectives to avoid these typical errors.

1. Choosing the Wrong State in Which to Register

Selecting the incorrect state for LLC formation might present considerable issues. Common errors include:

Not Considering Business Climate: Choosing a state primarily based on personal preferences rather than considering the business climate, tax structure, regulatory needs, and market dynamics.

Ignoring Tax Implications: Failing to examine state-specific tax requirements and advantages results in unanticipated tax bills or missing tax benefits.

Legal and compliance challenges: Registering in a state with complicated or rigorous legal requirements without comprehending the ramifications results in compliance challenges or administrative hassles.

Operational Limitations: Choosing a state that puts limits on corporate operations or lacks the resources required for the sector restricts growth and development.

Cost-Related Oversights: Overlooking cost implications linked with registration, yearly fees, taxes, and continuous compliance obligations in multiple states.

Disregarding Future Development Plans: Failing to evaluate the possibilities for company development into other states results in issues while operating in new territories.

Selecting the correct state for LLC registration takes a thorough examination of numerous variables to guarantee alignment with the business's goals, operational requirements, legal compliance, and future expansion plans.

1. Becoming Non-Compliant.

Non-compliance may significantly harm an LLC's business. Common errors leading to non-compliance include:

Regulatory Oversight: Failing to remain informed of new laws, rules, and compliance standards pertinent to the industry results in unintended infractions.

Missed files and deadlines: Neglecting to submit important paperwork, such as annual reports, taxes, or other compliance-related files, results in fines and legal implications.

Inadequate Record-Keeping: Poor documentation processes, including incomplete or incorrect records of meetings, transactions, or important company operations, result in compliance gaps.

Disregarding Licensing and Permits: Operating without acquiring or renewing essential licenses, permits, or certificates imposed by state or municipal authorities, incurring legal fines.

Misclassification of Employees: incorrectly identifying workers as independent contractors instead of employees, resulting in labor law infractions and associated fines.

Data Privacy and Security: Failing to conform to data protection standards, compromising consumer information, and exposing the organization to legal liability.

Maintaining compliance is crucial for an LLC's legitimacy and legal status. Staying educated, implementing rigorous record-keeping systems, and following all applicable legislation are crucial to preventing non-compliance difficulties.

1. Forming an LLC without the required licenses.

Forming an LLC without securing appropriate licenses and permissions might lead to legal and operational issues. Common errors include:

Lack of Research: Failing to perform extensive research to discover and secure the precise licenses and permissions necessary by the industry, location, or type of company activities.

Underestimating License Needs: Overlooking or underestimating the breadth of licenses, certificates, or permissions necessary for the company results in incomplete legal compliance.

Delay in Application: Waiting until after LLC creation to seek licenses and permissions, resulting in operational delays or legal penalties owing to the incapacity to execute specific commercial operations.

Inadequate Renewals: Neglecting to renew licenses or permits on time, causing delays to operations, and paying penalties or fines for operating with expired credentials.

Failure to Meet Industry Rules: Disregarding industry-specific rules and licensing requirements, which might result in non-compliance and subsequent legal proceedings.

Local Compliance Oversight: Ignoring local rules and regulations essential for operating a business inside a given city or area.

Acquiring the required licenses and permissions before initiating commercial activity is vital. It assures legal compliance, eliminates operational delays, and preserves the LLC's reputation within its industry and jurisdiction.

1. Not Getting the Correct Legal Assistance

Neglecting to get suitable legal assistance during LLC creation might lead to different issues. Common errors include:

Misinterpretation of Laws: Misunderstanding or misinterpreting complicated legal requirements and regulations, perhaps leading to non-compliance or lost opportunities.

Inadequate Knowledge: Lacking a full grasp of state-specific or industry-specific regulations may lead to unintended legal infractions or missing protections.

Poorly Drafted Papers: Creating legal papers, such as operating agreements, contracts, or compliance-related paperwork, without professional evaluation risks mistakes or omissions.

Overlooking Risk Management: Failing to handle possible legal risks or liabilities applicable to the industry or business strategy leaves the LLC open to legal conflicts.

Missing Legal Opportunities: not using legal counsel to optimize company structures, safeguard intellectual property, or rely on available legal solutions for development and protection.

Limited Understanding of Tax Consequences: Not appreciating the tax consequences of different company activities, leading to inefficient tax arrangements or unanticipated tax penalties.

Engaging skilled legal specialists assures full compliance, risk mitigation, and strategic assistance required for a firm foundation and the continuous success of the LLC.

1. Using Incorrect Documentation

Using the wrong paperwork during LLC creation or operations might lead to serious difficulties. Common errors include:

Template Errors: Relying on generic templates or outmoded forms that do not fit with particular state requirements or the LLC's unique needs, possibly leading to legal errors.

Inaccurate Information: Providing erroneous or missing facts in crucial papers like Articles of Organization or Operating Agreements might generate legal challenges or operational concerns.

Mismatched Agreements: Utilizing agreements or contracts that don't adequately represent the agreed terms among LLC members or with external parties, resulting in misunderstandings or problems.

Failure to Update Papers: Neglecting to update essential papers, such as operating agreements or bylaws, to reflect changes in the company structure or operational processes.

Non-compliance with State Requirements: Overlooking certain state requirements for document content or layout, resulting in rejection during filing procedures or future legal problems.

Lack of Professional evaluation: Failing to have legal or industry specialists evaluate essential papers, risking mistakes or omissions that may have been avoided with expert counsel.

Using accurate, up-to-date, and personalized paperwork evaluated by legal specialists is vital to maintaining legal compliance, limiting risks, and providing clear standards for the LLC's activities and interactions.

4.2 Mistakes to Avoid When Running an LLC

1. Not Having a Deadlock Provision in the Operating Agreement

Not having a stalemate clause in the operating agreement might offer major obstacles to an LLC's decision-making process. Common errors include:

Decision Impasse: Facing instances when members reach an impasse on crucial business choices, delaying development and possibly generating operational standstills.

Lack of Resolution Mechanism: Absence of a set means to resolve disputes or deadlocks among members, resulting in extended arguments and possible legal fights.

Impact on Company Operations: Inability to go ahead with crucial business choices, such as substantial investments, recruiting key individuals, or changes in company direction, impacting growth and stability.

Financial Consequences: Potential financial losses owing to delayed decision-making, lost opportunities, or lower investor trust stemming from internal disagreements.

Strained Relationships: Deadlocks may strain relationships among LLC members, resulting in greater stress, lower cooperation, and eventually harming the entire work environment.

Legal Vulnerabilities: Without a deadlock clause, arguments may develop into litigation, costing time and resources and compromising the LLC's reputation and financial stability.

Incorporating a deadlock clause in the operating agreement helps avoid these risks by specifying mechanisms to break impasses, providing smoother operations, clearer decision-making processes, and preserving the LLC's general functioning and development.

1. The Operating Agreement is Outdated

An obsolete operating agreement creates several hazards and issues for an LLC. Common errors connected to this include:

Incompatibility with Current Operations: An outmoded agreement could not correspond with the contemporary corporate structure, strategy, or goals, leading to uncertainty among members regarding their roles and duties.

Legal Inaccuracy: Changes in laws or regulations could make the agreement non-compliant or insufficient, thereby exposing the LLC to legal risks or litigation.

Unclear Decision-Making Protocols: Modifications in ownership, profit distribution, voting rights, or management structures not represented in the agreement might cause conflicts or ambiguity in decision-making procedures.

Lack of Protection: Failure to update terms about liability, dispute resolution, or member rights might leave the LLC open to unanticipated dangers or conflicts.

Misleading Documentation: An obsolete agreement could mislead the actual situation of the firm to external parties, including investors, partners, or stakeholders.

Missed Opportunities: Failing to amend the agreement might mean losing out on enhancing the LLC's structure or adopting new legal tactics useful for development or protection.

Regularly evaluating and revising the operating agreement ensures that it appropriately represents the LLC's actual situation, mitigates legal concerns, and offers clarity and alignment among members, establishing a favorable atmosphere for development and stability.

1. Members Do Not Properly Document LLC Activity

When members fail to properly record LLC actions, it may lead to different operational and legal difficulties. Common errors related to this include:

Lack of Financial Clarity: Inadequate record-keeping of financial activities, including income, costs, and investments, may result in confused financial statements, making it hard to analyze the company's financial health properly.

Compliance Issues: Incomplete or faulty paperwork may lead to non-compliance with tax rules, reporting requirements, or other legal duties, subjecting the LLC to fines or audits.

Loss of company insights: Insufficient documentation might restrict the capacity to assess company performance, make educated choices, or monitor the efficacy of plans, thereby hindering growth chances.

Difficulty in Dispute Settlement: Incomplete records might impede the settlement of internal disputes or conflicts among members about financial concerns or operational choices.

chance of mismanagement: Without sufficient documentation of LLC operations, there's a larger chance of mismanagement, including difficulties relating to financial transparency, accountability, and decision-making procedures.

Impact on Credibility: Inadequate paperwork may impair the LLC's credibility when interacting with external stakeholders, such as investors, lenders, or regulatory agencies, thus hurting business relationships or prospects.

Maintaining accurate and thorough records of LLC operations is vital for compliance, transparency, informed decision-making, and safeguarding the general health and legitimacy of the organization.

1. Mixing company funds with personal funds.

Mixing corporate cash with personal finances may lead to many issues inside an LLC. Common errors related to this activity include:
Legal Liability Concerns: Blurring the borders between personal and corporate money might undermine the limited liability protection normally afforded by an LLC. This might expose personal assets to business-related liabilities or legal claims.
Tax Implications: Combining money might make it tough to identify corporate costs from personal ones, resulting in complications during tax filings, possible IRS audits, or the loss of tax deductions.
Financial Confusion: Merging funds may produce financial turmoil, making it impossible to analyze firm revenue, costs, profits, or losses effectively, leading to erroneous financial reporting and decision-making.
Undermining Professional Image: Intermingling money could give an unprofessional image to stakeholders, including clients, partners, or investors, undermining the credibility and reliability of the LLC.
Complex Accounting: Mixing money may complicate bookkeeping and accounting operations, making it tough to generate the correct financial statements or reports required for corporate evaluations or audits.
Operational Challenges: It might generate issues in managing cash flow, budgeting, or forecasting appropriately, hampering the LLC's ability to plan and execute business initiatives efficiently.

Maintaining a significant distinction between personal and corporate funds is vital for sustaining limited liability protection, assuring proper financial management, and maintaining the professionalism and integrity of the LLC.

CHAPTER FIVE

CONVERTING YOUR EXISTING BUSINESS INTO AN LLC

5.1 What Kind of Businesses Can Be Converted into LLCs?

1. Sole Proprietorship.

Sole proprietorships are among the most frequent company types that may be changed into Limited Liability Companies (LLCs). Here are some crucial elements to consider:

Sole Proprietorship to LLC: Transitioning from a sole proprietorship to an LLC provides for a transition from personal responsibility to limited liability protection. It isolates personal assets from corporate debts and commitments, safeguarding personal finances from business hazards.

Simplicity in Conversion: Converting a single proprietorship to an LLC is pretty uncomplicated. The procedure entails submitting articles of formation, acquiring a new Employer Identification Number (EIN), and restructuring corporate accounts.

Continuity of Business Operations: The conversion preserves business continuity, enabling smooth operations under the LLC form without major interruption to current customers, contracts, or activities.

Tax Considerations: The move to an LLC may affect tax responsibilities. While a single proprietor declares company revenue on personal tax returns, an LLC may select how it's taxed: as a disregarded entity (like a sole proprietorship), a partnership, an S corporation, or a C corporation.

Enhanced Credibility: Operating as an LLC may boost credibility with customers, partners, or prospective investors since it suggests a more official and organized corporate organization.

Converting a sole proprietorship to an LLC may provide several advantages, including liability protection and a more structured corporate structure, perhaps opening the way for future growth and expansion.

1. Corporation.

Converting a company into a Limited Liability Company (LLC) includes numerous considerations:

Differences in Structure: Corporations often have a more complicated organizational structure with shareholders, a board of directors, and officials. An LLC, in contrast, provides a simpler form with flexibility in administration.

Tax Implications: Corporations are susceptible to double taxation, where the business is taxed on earnings, and shareholders are taxed on dividends. Converting to an LLC may prevent this double taxation by enabling the LLC's revenues and losses to flow through to the members' tax returns.

Legal Formalities: Corporations have severe compliance obligations, including frequent shareholder meetings, formal record-keeping, and paperwork. Converting to an LLC may give relief from some of these requirements, enabling a more flexible operating environment.

Liability Protection: Both corporations and LLCs provide limited liability protection, but an LLC often allows greater freedom in managing and sharing earnings while keeping this protection.

Conversion Process: The conversion process entails submitting articles of incorporation for the LLC and, in certain situations, receiving approval from shareholders and meeting state-specific procedures.

influence on Contracts and Agreements: The move to an LLC can influence current contracts, agreements, or connections with customers, suppliers, or partners. It's crucial to evaluate these agreements to guarantee a seamless transition.

Converting from a corporation to an LLC might bring operational flexibility, streamlined management structures, and possible tax advantages, but it needs a thorough examination of legal, tax, and operational factors before making the transfer.

1. LLC Groups.

The notion of LLC groups applies to the structuring of many LLCs under a united organization. When contemplating turning many LLCs into an LLC group, various variables come into play:

Unified administration: An LLC group enables for centralized administration and coordination of numerous LLCs, promoting a more coherent approach to corporate operations.

Asset Protection: Segregating separate assets or lines of business into independent LLCs within a group gives an extra degree of protection. It safeguards one LLC's assets from the obligations or hazards linked with another.

Operational Flexibility: Each LLC within the group may keep its autonomy while benefitting from common resources, centralized administration, or collaborative decision-making, boosting operational efficiency.

Tax Implications: An LLC group may have various tax benefits, such as sharing losses and earnings among the LLCs. This structure also gives flexibility in how the LLCs are taxed, allowing for tax optimization tactics.

Regulatory Compliance: Forming an LLC group includes compliance with state legislation, ensuring that each LLC within the group functions in line with the unique legal requirements.

Complexity in Management: Managing several LLCs within a group may be difficult, requiring excellent communication, a clear definition of tasks, and well-structured governance to prevent disputes or misunderstandings.

Forming an LLC group includes strategic planning, legal considerations, and a clear grasp of the business's overarching goals to harness the advantages of collective management while preserving individual entities within the group.

5.2 Advantages and Disadvantages of Changing Your Business an LLC

Converting an existing firm into a Limited Liability Company (LLC) provides several benefits and drawbacks, impacting the decision-making process:

Advantages

Limited Liability: The key benefit is insulating personal assets from company responsibilities. Owners' assets are often safeguarded in case of commercial debts or legal proceedings against the organization.

Tax Flexibility: LLCs provide flexibility in taxes, enabling owners to choose between pass-through taxation (like a partnership or sole proprietorship) or opting to be taxed as a corporation for possible tax savings.

Operational freedom: Compared to corporations, LLCs have less formality, such as fewer continuing compliance obligations, low paperwork, and fewer meetings, offering greater freedom in day-to-day operations.

Ownership Structure: LLCs offer a more adjustable ownership structure, enabling multiple sorts of members (individuals, companies, other LLCs, etc.), allowing for diversified ownership arrangements.

Disadvantages

Limited Growth future: While LLCs provide several benefits, they could have difficulties in recruiting investors owing to a less structured structure compared to corporations, which might hinder future growth and financing prospects.

State-Specific Requirements: State laws regulating LLCs differ, and compliance with these requirements could add complexity to operations, particularly if the firm operates in numerous jurisdictions.

Tax Complexity: While LLCs give tax freedom, the choice of taxation and the distribution of earnings among members may occasionally lead to tax complications, requiring careful planning and knowledge of tax rules.

Perceived Credibility: Some sectors or clientele could regard corporations as more established or reliable compared to LLCs, thereby influencing business relationships.

Considering these pros and cons might help company owners make an educated choice when contemplating the transfer of their present business structure to an LLC.

5.3 Procedure to Convert Your Sole Proprietorship to an LLC

When changing a single proprietorship to a Limited Liability Company (LLC), many critical processes need to be followed:

1. Confirm the Name of Your Business:

Check Availability: Ensure that the selected company name is available and consistent with your state's LLC naming requirements. The name should normally be recognizable from existing businesses in your state and should include the term "LLC" or its complete form, depending on state laws.

Reserve the Name (if necessary): Some jurisdictions enable the reserve of a company name for a set time before actually establishing the LLC. If needed or if you predict a delay in registration, consider reserving the selected company name.

Check Domain Availability: If you want to establish an online presence, check the availability of the matching domain name for your company website.

complete Name reserve (if required): If your state needs name reserve or registration, complete the relevant papers with the appropriate state office to acquire the selected company name.

Confirming the company name is the first stage in the process of changing from a single proprietorship to an LLC. It establishes the groundwork for the legal creation of your new company organization while assuring compliance with state legislation regulating business names.

1. File Articles of Organization.

When converting from a single proprietorship to a Limited Liability Company (LLC), submitting the Articles of Organization is a critical step. Here's a breakdown of the process:

Obtain the Form: Acquire the Articles of Organization form from the Secretary of State or comparable state office responsible for company registrations.

Complete the Form: Fill out the Articles of Organization form with precise and relevant information. This normally contains facts such as the LLC name, company location, registered agent information, member or management details, and the LLC's purpose.

Submit the Form: File the completed Articles of Organization form with the relevant state agency. Alongside the form, pay the appropriate filing fee, which varies by state.

Publication Requirements (if applicable): In certain states, LLCs are obliged to publish a notice of its establishment in local media. Ensure compliance with any publishing obligations enforced by the state.

Wait for Approval: After submission, the state agency will evaluate the papers. Once accepted, you'll get proof of the LLC's creation, frequently in the form of a Certificate of Organization or equivalent document.

Operating Agreement: While not usually required by the state, establishing an Operating Agreement defining the internal operations, ownership, and management structure of the LLC is desirable. This agreement is needed for clarity among members and for legal protection.

Filing the Articles of Organization legally creates your LLC as a distinct company organization, giving liability protection and official acknowledgment of the change from a sole proprietorship to an LLC. It's a critical phase in the process and establishes the basis for your new company structure.

1. Draft Your Operating Agreement.

Drafting an Operating Agreement is a vital component of transforming a single proprietorship into a Limited Liability Company (LLC). Here's a guide to the process:

Understand its Importance: An Operating Agreement is a contract that specifies the internal workings, management structure, member responsibilities, and operational parameters of the LLC. Although not usually needed by state law, having one is strongly suggested to designate crucial components of the firm.

Content of the Agreement: The Operating Agreement should incorporate crucial components such as member duties and responsibilities, ownership percentages, decision-making methods, profit distribution, regulations for adding or removing members, dissolution procedures, and dispute resolution systems.

Consultation and Legal Assistance: Consider getting legal counsel or consulting with a professional versed in business law to verify the operating agreement matches your company goals, complies with state laws, and protects the interests of all concerned parties.

Customization: Tailor the Operating Agreement to meet your business objectives and the nature of your LLC. This contract gives freedom in organizing the firm as per the choices and demands of the members.

Unanimous Consent: Ensure that all members properly comprehend and agree upon the provisions specified in the Operating Agreement before completing and signing it. Unanimous consensus among members helps avoid problems or misunderstandings down the road.

Storage and Accessibility: Once completed and signed by all members, keep the Operating Agreement in a secure and accessible area. It should be easily accessible for reference and evaluation whenever required.

Drafting an Operating Agreement serves as a critical step in formalizing the internal structure and activities of your freshly created LLC. It's a proactive effort to provide clarity, minimize misconceptions, and maintain seamless working among members.

1. Tax Compliance.

When moving your firm from a single proprietorship to a Limited Liability Company (LLC), adhering to tax compliance is vital. Here's a guide:

EIN Application: Obtain an Employer Identification Number (EIN) from the Internal Revenue Service (IRS) for your LLC. The EIN acts as a unique identity for tax reasons and is necessary for numerous financial activities, recruiting personnel, and creating a company bank account.

Tax Classification: Determine the tax classification for your LLC. By default, a single-member LLC is taxed as a disregarded entity (like a sole proprietorship) or as a partnership for multi-member LLCs. Alternatively, LLCs may opt to be taxed as a corporation (C-corp or S-corp) by completing the proper documents with the IRS.

Tax Reporting: Understand the tax reporting requirements for your selected tax categorization. For example, sole proprietorships and partnerships submit Schedule C or K-1 correspondingly with their tax returns, whereas corporations have separate tax filings using Form 1120 or 1120-S.

State Tax Duties: Be mindful of state tax duties. Depending on the state in which the LLC operates, there can be state-specific taxes, such as income tax, sales tax, or franchise tax. Ensure compliance with these state-level tax rules.

projected Taxes: Plan for and make projected tax payments if required. LLC members typically need to make quarterly estimated tax payments to offset income tax obligations not covered by withholding.

Record-Keeping: Maintain accurate and complete financial records, including income, spending, payroll records (if applicable), and any other financial activities relating to the LLC. Organized records speed up tax preparation and aid in establishing conformity during audits.

Tax Professional Consultation: Seek guidance from a tax professional or accountant acquainted with small business taxes. Their knowledge may assist with tax-saving techniques, deductions, and compliance, guaranteeing correct adherence to tax rules and regulations.

Maintaining tax compliance is crucial to the business and legal status of your LLC. By remaining informed and executing your duties immediately and properly, you create the framework for a smooth and compliant tax journey for your firm.

1. Open a Bank Account

When changing your single proprietorship into a Limited Liability Company (LLC), setting up a separate company bank account is vital. Here's what you should consider:

Choose the Right Bank: Select a bank that meets your company's demands. Consider variables including prices, account features, location, internet banking alternatives, and extra services specialized for small companies.

Gather Required documentation: Prepare the essential documentation to establish the business account. These normally contain your EIN, LLC formation paperwork (Articles of Organization), company license, and personal identity (such as driver's license or passport).

Business Structure Verification: The bank can want documentation of your LLC's existence. Provide the Articles of Organization or other applicable state-issued papers to demonstrate the validity of your company.

Separate money: Emphasize the need to separate personal and company money. A specialized company account enables obvious segregation of money, simplifies bookkeeping, and enhances the limited liability protection given by the LLC form.

Merchant Services and Extra Features: Inquire about extra services the bank provides, such as merchant services, business credit cards, lines of credit, or online payment solutions. These may speed transactions and enhance your business's financial operations.

Initial Deposit: Be prepared to make an initial deposit as needed by the bank to activate the account. Some banks could have minimum balance requirements or particular deposit amounts to start the account.

Understand Account Terms: Carefully understand the terms and conditions of the business account. Understand fees, transaction limitations, overdraft protection, and any other account-related particulars before concluding the opening procedure.

Regular Account Maintenance: Once the account is open, maintain regular monitoring and maintenance. Keep accurate records of transactions, reconcile statements, and be informed of account activity to prevent any inconsistencies or possible difficulties.

Establishing a distinct business bank account for your LLC is a vital step toward handling money independently, assuring transparency, and allowing seamless financial operations for your organization.

1. Apply for your business license.

When changing your single proprietorship to a limited liability company (LLC), getting the proper business licenses is vital for legal compliance. Here's a tutorial on how to tackle this:

Identify Required Licenses: Research and identify the exact business licenses and permits required for your LLC. Requirements vary depending on your industry, region, and the nature of your company's activity. Contact your local government, municipal, or county offices to determine the appropriate permissions.

Check State and municipal rules: Understand the rules controlling your industry at both the state and municipal levels. Each country can have distinct licensing needs, so verify you comply with all necessary rules.

Application Process: Obtain the relevant application forms from the authorized authorities. Complete the application correctly and supply any needed paperwork, which may include your LLC's Articles of Organization, business strategy, evidence of insurance, or zoning compliance.

costs and durations: Be mindful of related costs and processing durations. Some licenses demand payment of application fees, renewal fees, or periodic inspections. Ensure timely submission to prevent any delays in approval.

Follow-up and Compliance: After filing your application, follow up with the licensing authorities periodically. Ensure compliance with any extra requirements or adjustments they may seek and swiftly handle any lingering problems or concerns.

Maintain License Renewals: Once your company license is approved, maintain a note of its expiration date. Renew the license before its expiration to maintain compliance and prevent fines or business problems.

Display Your License: Once received, prominently display your business license at your place of operation as allowed by local legislation. This enables openness and compliance during any inspections or inquiries.

Stay Informed: Stay informed on any changes in rules or new requirements that could affect your company. Compliance with licensing regulations is a continual duty for your LLC.

By getting the proper company licenses and complying with local rules, you guarantee that your LLC runs lawfully and avoids possible fines or interruptions due to non-compliance. It's a key step in establishing your company and developing trust with consumers and authorities.

5.4 Procedure to Convert Your Corporation to an LLC

1. Create a Conversion Plan

When converting a corporation to a limited liability company (LLC), developing a clear conversion strategy is vital for a successful transfer. Here's an overview of the process:

Evaluation of Business Structure: Assess and identify why the conversion to an LLC is the recommended solution. Consider variables such as taxes, liability protection, managerial flexibility, and operational needs.

Legal Considerations: Review the legal ramifications of the conversion. Consult legal and financial professionals to understand the legal processes, tax repercussions, and regulatory requirements involved in moving from a corporation to an LLC.

Modify Articles of Organization/Incorporation: Prepare and submit the appropriate papers to modify the corporation's Articles of Incorporation to Articles of Organization for the LLC. This can entail preparing and submitting Articles of Conversion or Articles of Organization, depending on your state's requirements.

Approval by Shareholders/Board of Directors: Obtain approval for the conversion from the corporation's shareholders or board of directors, as needed by state laws and the corporation's bylaws.

Transfer of Assets and Liabilities: Transfer assets and liabilities from the company to the newly established LLC. This can include amending contracts, leases, licenses, and bank accounts under the LLC's name.

Tax Considerations: Understand the tax consequences of the conversion. Ensure conformity with tax rules, and if applicable, get an Employer Identification Number (EIN) for the LLC. Consult with tax specialists to manage tax filings and guarantee a seamless transition.

Conversion timetable and implementation: Develop a timetable describing the processes involved in the conversion process.

Allocate resources, assign duties, and create timeframes to facilitate a smooth transition from corporation to LLC.

Legal Compliance and Filings: Complete all essential documentation and filings with the state authorities. This can entail submitting Articles of Conversion, amending registrations, and getting appropriate permissions or licenses for the newly constituted LLC.

Notification to Stakeholders: Notify customers, suppliers, workers, and other important stakeholders about the conversion. Update company contracts, agreements, and communication materials to reflect the move from a corporation to an LLC.

Post-conversion evaluation: After the conversion, do a detailed evaluation to verify all components of the transition are finished. Confirm that all assets, contracts, licenses, and agreements are correctly transferred to the LLC.

Developing a detailed conversion strategy helps speed the process, reduces interruptions, and assures compliance with legal and regulatory requirements when moving your company to an LLC. Consulting legal and financial specialists may give useful insight along this conversion path.

1. Shareholder Approval is Required

Securing shareholder approval is a vital step when turning a company into a Limited Liability Company (LLC). Here's a summary of the shareholder approval procedure as part of the conversion plan:

Review Corporate Bylaws/Operating Agreement: Examine the corporation's bylaws to discover the exact procedures for getting shareholder approval for the conversion. The bylaws could describe the methods and vote thresholds required for this decision.

Schedule a Shareholder Meeting: Organize and schedule a meeting of the corporation's shareholders. Provide prior notification as required by state legislation and the corporation's bylaws. Offer full information regarding the planned conversion, its advantages, and implications.

Presentation of Conversion Plan: Present the proposed conversion plan at the shareholder meeting. Include facts on why the conversion is favorable, the legal procedures involved, possible tax advantages, and the effect on shareholders' interests.

Discussion and Voting: Facilitate a discussion enabling shareholders to raise questions and express their concerns or support for the conversion. Then hold a formal vote. Depending on the rules, the vote could be by a simple majority or need a particular percentage of acceptance.

Documenting the Resolution: If the shareholders vote in favor of the conversion, record the resolution or decision taken at the meeting.

Record the specifics of the approval, including the number of votes in favor and any opposing votes or abstentions.

Filing the Resolution: File the authorized resolution or decision with the company records and applicable state authorities. Ensure compliance with state legislation surrounding the conversion process and shareholder approval paperwork.

amend Records and Agreements: After getting shareholder approval, amend corporate records, agreements, and any other legal documents to reflect the decision to convert the company to an LLC. By receiving shareholder approval, the organization may move confidently with the conversion process while guaranteeing openness and compliance with corporate governance rules. It's a vital step in expressing the support of the company's stakeholders in this strategic transformation.

1. File the Correct Documents.

When changing a corporation into a Limited Liability Company (LLC), completing the necessary documentation is important for a flawless transfer. Here's a summary of the important stages needed in submitting the proper documentation for the conversion:

Articles of Conversion or Articles of Organization: Depending on the state's requirements, create and submit the relevant papers. This can require submitting Articles of Conversion if available or Articles of Organization to create the LLC.

State-specific Forms and Applications: Identify and complete state-specific forms and applications necessary for the conversion. Each state has its own rules, therefore guaranteeing compliance with their unique filing needs.

revised Operating Agreement or Bylaws: Draft a revised Operating Agreement for the LLC or update the corporation's bylaws to reflect the decision to convert. This paper contains the rules and regulations governing the new organization.

Tax Identification Number (EIN) Application: If the LLC needs a new Employer Identification Number (EIN), submit an application for a new EIN to the Internal Revenue Service (IRS).

Business Licenses and Permits: Update or get essential business licenses, permits, or registrations for the newly created LLC. Ensure compliance with local, state, and federal requirements.

Transfer of Intellectual Property and Contracts: If relevant, secure the correct transfer or assignment of intellectual property rights, contracts, leases, and agreements from the corporation to the LLC.

Additional Filings (if required): Some states may need additional filings or notifications relating to the conversion, such as notifications to creditors or posting notices in local newspapers.

Filing Fees and Dates: Submit the filings together with the relevant fees to the appropriate state agency within the stipulated dates to prevent any delays in the conversion process.

Confirmation and Documentation: Once the papers are submitted, acquire confirmations, receipts, or acknowledgments from the proper authorities. Keep copies of all submitted paperwork and confirmations for business records.

Professional Consultation: Consider getting help from legal and financial consultants specialized in company conversions to guarantee accuracy and compliance with state legislation throughout the filing process.

Filing the right paperwork precisely and within the required times is vital for completing the change from a corporation to an LLC. It sets the legal basis and formalizes the new entity's structure and activities.

Chapter Six

Accounting for Your LLC

6.1 What is a general ledger and what does it record?

1. LLC Investment Assets

Certainly! When addressing the accounting component of an LLC, knowing the general ledger and its function in documenting numerous elements is crucial.

The general ledger for an LLC gathers and categorizes a spectrum of financial operations, including investment assets. Here's a summary of the function of the general ledger addressing LLC investment assets:

Asset Recording: Investment assets, such as stocks, bonds, real estate holdings, or any other type of investments made by the LLC, are scrupulously documented inside the general ledger.

Identification and Classification: Each investment asset is identified and classed inside the ledger. This categorization method comprises providing unique IDs or identities and identifying the nature of the investment for clear and orderly tracking.

Valuation and Tracking: The ledger continually keeps records of the value and changes in the investment assets. It monitors swings in their value, any revenue earned (dividends or interest), and the accompanying costs or losses incurred.

Accounting Entries: Entries linked to the purchase, sale, or liquidation of investment assets are precisely noted in the ledger. This comprises original purchase expenses, future transactions, appreciation or depreciation, and any related fees or commissions.

Financial Reporting: Information from the general ledger about investment assets is vital for developing accurate financial reports. It assists in measuring the overall financial health, performance, and value of the LLC.

Compliance & Auditing: The ledger offers a record of all investment-related operations, simplifying compliance with regulatory standards and aiding auditing procedures. It guarantees openness and accountability in the LLC's financial activities.

Decision Making: Reliable and up-to-date information on investment assets produced from the ledger supports stakeholders, management, and investors in making educated choices about the LLC's investment strategy and future directions.

Maintaining a complete and well-organized general ledger is crucial for an LLC. It provides for rigorous monitoring, analysis, and reporting of investment assets, allowing the LLC to manage its financial portfolio efficiently and make strategic choices under its goals.

1. Equipment

Certainly! Within the area of accounting for an LLC, the general ledger serves a critical function in monitoring numerous assets, including equipment.

The general ledger documents and monitors the equipment held by the LLC, guaranteeing accurate and orderly documentation of these assets. Here's an overview of how the general ledger controls equipment:

Asset Identification: Equipment, such as equipment, automobiles, computers, or other physical assets employed by the LLC for company activities, is recognized and reported inside the ledger.

Procurement and prices: Details concerning the procurement of equipment, including purchase prices, installation expenditures, and any extra costs related to putting the equipment into operational use, are painstakingly noted in the ledger.

Depreciation and amortization: The general ledger accounts for the depreciation or amortization of equipment during its useful life. This entails deliberately spreading out the cost of the equipment over time to reflect its lower worth due to wear and tear or obsolescence.

Maintenance and Repairs: Any expenses made for maintaining, repairing, or upgrading the equipment are noted in the ledger. These inputs contribute to establishing the total operating expenses connected with the device.

Disposal or Sale: When equipment is disposed of, sold, or retired from service, related entries describing the sale profits, write-offs, or any gains or losses from the transaction are entered in the ledger.
Regulatory Compliance: Accurate and thorough records inside the ledger provide compliance with accounting standards and regulatory obligations connected to equipment accounting and reporting.
Financial Reporting: Information from the ledger about equipment assets is used to produce financial statements, including balance sheets, income statements, and cash flow statements. It gives insights into the value and utilization of the LLC's equipment assets.
Management Decision Support: The ledger's data about equipment enables management to analyze the efficiency of equipment utilization, plan for replacements or upgrades, and make educated choices regarding capital expenditures on new equipment.
The precise recording and monitoring of equipment inside the general ledger permit full asset management for the LLC. It guarantees that correct information is accessible for financial reporting, compliance, and strategic decision-making linked to the usage and upkeep of equipment assets.

1. Income and Expenditure

Absolutely! Within an LLC's accounting system, the general ledger is crucial in supervising the revenue and spending streams.

Money Records: The general ledger methodically details all sources of money produced by the LLC. This comprises income from sales, services supplied, interest, dividends, or any other type of profit related to the company's activity.

Expenditure Tracking: It tracks all costs spent by the LLC in the course of its activities. This comprises costs linked to raw materials, labor, rent, utilities, advertising, administrative expenses, taxes, interest payments, and any other operational or capital expenditures.

Categorization and Classification: Income and spending items are sorted and categorized inside the ledger to assist in structured tracking and analysis. This classification frequently fits with normal accounting processes and guarantees accurate allocation to specified spending or revenue groups.

Timing and Accrual: The ledger accounts for revenue and costs based on accrual or cash accounting procedures, depending on the LLC's selected accounting style. Accrual accounting captures revenue and costs as they are generated or incurred, irrespective of when the cash transactions occur. Cash accounting, on the other hand, recognizes revenue and costs only when cash changes hands.

Financial Reporting: The data from the ledger about revenue and spending creates the basis for financial reports like income statements or profit and loss statements. These reports give insights into the LLC's financial performance, including sales, costs, and net profitability over a specific period of time.

Study and Decision Making: Accurate entries in the ledger allow extensive study of revenue sources and spending trends. This study supports budgeting, cost management, and strategic decision-making, enabling the LLC to optimize its financial resources and maximize profitability.

Compliance and Auditing: Detailed records in the ledger help comply with tax legislation and accounting standards. They also assist audits by giving a clear trail of revenue and spending, enabling openness and accountability in financial processes.

The thorough recording and monitoring of revenue and spending inside the general ledger serve as a crucial part of an LLC's financial management. It gives a comprehensive perspective of the business's financial health, supporting strategic planning, compliance, and decision-making processes.

6.2 Best Method of Taxation

1. Partnership.

Taxation techniques for an LLC play a significant part in its financial structure. Let's look into the intricacies of one prevalent taxing method:

Pass-Through Taxation: In a partnership taxation arrangement for an LLC, the company itself does not pay income tax at the entity level. Instead, the earnings and losses "pass through" the LLC to its members (owners).

Form 1065: Partnerships file IRS Form 1065, which offers an informative return reflecting each partner's portion of earnings, losses, deductions, and credits. However, the real tax burden is declared and paid by individual partners on their tax returns.

Allocation of Income and Losses: Partnerships have the option to share income and losses differently among partners, depending on the parameters established in the LLC's operating agreement or partnership agreement.

Self-Employment Taxes: Partners in an LLC are liable for self-employment taxes on their portion of the earnings, which cover Social Security and Medicare taxes. This tax rate might be greater than the rate for workers, since partners are liable for both the employer and employee shares of these taxes.

Deductions and Tax Credits: Partnerships give numerous tax deductions and credits to partners, which they may claim on their tax returns. This can include deductions for company costs, retirement plan contributions, healthcare bills, and other qualified things.

Tax Planning and Reporting: Partners in a partnership must carefully examine tax planning tactics, given the flexibility in dividing revenue and losses. This might entail optimizing deductions, regulating the timing of income recognition, and maintaining compliance with IRS requirements.

Quarterly Estimated Taxes: Partners often make quarterly estimated tax payments to satisfy their tax responsibilities throughout the year, considering their share of earnings earned by the LLC.

Complexity and Legal Guidance: Partnership taxes may become complicated owing to varied allocations, distributions, and tax consequences. Seeking expert guidance from tax accountants or lawyers versed in partnership taxes is frequently essential to guarantee compliance and the best tax strategies.

Understanding partnership taxes inside an LLC is critical for members to make educated choices regarding tax planning, revenue distribution, and overall financial management strategies. It provides advantages in terms of flexibility and tax treatment, although it demands careful preparation and adherence to tax restrictions for the best outcomes.

1. Sole Proprietorship

Certainly, in the context of taxes, running an LLC as a sole proprietorship might provide unique benefits and considerations:

Pass-Through Taxation: Similar to partnership taxation, a sole proprietorship LLC doesn't pay separate income taxes. Instead, all revenues and losses "pass through" the firm to the owner's tax return.

Tax Reporting on Schedule C: Sole Proprietorship LLCs submit a Schedule C (Profit or Loss from Business) together with their tax return (Form 1040). This form covers the business's revenue, costs, and net profit or loss.

Self-Employment Taxes: Sole proprietors are liable for self-employment taxes, including Social Security and Medicare taxes. The tax rate could be higher for workers owing to this dual duty.

Tax Deductions and Credits: Sole proprietors are entitled to several tax deductions, such as company costs, home office deductions, retirement plan contributions, and healthcare expenses. Additionally, they may claim certain tax benefits relating to their firm.

Quarterly Estimated Taxes: Sole Proprietors often make quarterly estimated tax payments to fulfill their tax responsibilities since they don't have taxes taken from regular paychecks.

Tax Compliance and Reporting: Compliance with IRS requirements and proper reporting of company revenue and expenditures are vital. Maintaining detailed records and receipts is vital for correct tax reporting.

Tax Planning and Strategies: Sole Proprietors should deliberate tax planning to maximize deductions, reduce tax payments, and manage tax rates efficiently. Consulting with a tax expert may help uncover possible deductions and design tax-efficient methods.

Responsibility Considerations: Although not directly connected to taxes, it's crucial to know that although sole proprietors enjoy pass-through taxation, they're also individually accountable for company debts and responsibilities, unlike some alternative business structures that give limited responsibility.

Operating as a sole proprietorship under an LLC form may simplify tax reporting and allow some flexibility. However, it's vital to balance the tax advantages with the individual's liability exposure and the overall financial demands of the organization. Professional assistance is required to make educated judgments and comply with tax requirements.

1. Corporation

Operating an LLC taxed as a corporation (C-Corp or S-Corp) implies various tax issues and advantages:

C-Corporation Taxation:

Double Taxation: C-Corps are subject to double taxation, whereby the corporation pays taxes on its income and shareholders pay taxes on dividends received.

Corporation Tax Rate: C-Corps are taxed at the corporation tax rate, which may vary depending on taxable income. Recent tax revisions brought modifications to business tax rates.

Retained profits: The C-Corp form enables the accumulation of profits inside the firm to finance development, expansion, or investment.

S-Corporation Taxation:

Pass-Through Taxation: Similar to partnerships and sole proprietorships, S-Corps do not pay corporation income tax. Instead, income and losses "pass-through" to shareholders' tax returns.

Avoiding Double Taxation: Shareholders record their portion of S-Corp revenue on their tax returns, avoiding the double taxation burden of C-Corps.

Self-Employment Taxes: S-Corp stockholders could get fair remuneration and pay payroll taxes on that amount, but additional distributions may not be subject to self-employment taxes.

Tax Reporting and Compliance:

Both C-Corps and S-Corps have unique tax reporting obligations, including submitting yearly tax returns (Form 1120 for C-Corps, Form 1120S for S-Corps) and reporting dividends, income, deductions, and credits.

Proper paperwork, precise financial accounts, and compliance with IRS laws are vital for both kinds of organizations.

Tax Deductions and Benefits:

Both kinds of companies may claim different tax deductions for genuine company expenditures, including wages, operational expenses, healthcare benefits, and some eligible business deductions.

Deductions and advantages may change depending on the organizational structure; thus, contact with a tax specialist is advised.

Tax Planning and Strategies:

Corporations may apply tax planning tactics to maximize deductions, credits, and tax advantages available for their unique form of company.

Strategies could include optimizing deductions, assessing the timing of costs and income, seeking tax credits, and controlling taxable events.

Operating as a company under an LLC form may give significant tax advantages, but it demands compliance with complicated tax rules and regulations. A careful assessment of the business's financial objectives and consultation with a tax specialist is necessary to ensure compliance and optimize tax benefits.

6.3 Choosing the Best Accounting System.

1. Accrual Basis Accounting

Accrual basis accounting and cash basis accounting are two basic approaches used to record and report financial transactions inside an LLC.

Recognition of Transactions:

Recognizes income when it's generated and costs when it's spent, irrespective of when currency trades hands.

Records transactions when the obligation occurs or when goods or services are given, independent of payment dates.

Accurate financial picture:

Provides a more accurate representation of a company's financial health by matching revenue and spending to the time they occur, delivering a more thorough snapshot of the company's financial status.

Complexity and Accuracy:

It can be more complicated to manage since it involves careful monitoring of accounts receivable, accounts payable, and accrued costs to assure correctness.

Offers a more realistic portrayal of a company's financial position, particularly for larger organizations or those engaging in major credit transactions.

Compliance and Reporting:

Generally needed for bigger organizations or entities that provide credit or have inventory, and frequently essential for compliance considerations, such as fulfilling Generally Accepted Accounting Principles (GAAP) regulations.

Long-Term Financial Analysis:

It allows for improved long-term financial monitoring since it correctly portrays the company's financial performance over time, despite cash flow variations.

Choosing between accrual and cash-based accounting frequently relies on the size of the organization, its industry, and legal constraints. For an LLC, particularly one with greater revenues, a complicated business, or several investors, accrual basis accounting may give a more complete perspective of financial health, assisting in improved decision-making and compliance. However, it needs precise record-keeping and a deep comprehension of financial fundamentals. Consulting with an accountant or financial expert is suggested to identify the best match for your LLC's unique requirements.

1. Cash Basis Accounting

Cash basis accounting is an accounting approach that records transactions only when cash exchanges hands, either received or spent.

Recognition of Transactions:

Records income when cash is received and costs when cash is paid out, regardless of when the revenue was produced or the expense spent.

Simpler than accrual accounting since it immediately represents cash flow, making it simpler to comprehend and apply.

Simplicity and Ease:

Simpler to manage and appropriate for smaller organizations or those with basic transactions.

Suitable for firms with less sophisticated financial arrangements and limited credit transactions.

Limited financial picture:

It might not fully indicate a company's financial health since it doesn't address accounts receivable, accounts payable, or accrued costs.

Can skew financial results, particularly for organizations that extend credit or have large non-cash activities.

Compliance and Reporting:

It's often utilized for tax reporting reasons, particularly for smaller enterprises, since it's easier and less resource-intensive.

Not suited for firms obliged to conform to Generally Accepted Accounting Principles (GAAP) requirements or those who need a thorough financial overview.

Short-Term Financial Analysis:

Provides a more immediate grasp of cash flow and liquidity but may not provide a full insight into long-term financial health or performance.

Cash-based accounting is comparatively easy to execute and ideal for smaller, uncomplicated enterprises that deal solely with cash transactions. However, it could not provide the depth of financial insights necessary for bigger, more sophisticated firms or those hoping for thorough financial reporting and analysis. The decision between cash and accrual basis accounting generally relies on the type and magnitude of the LLC's activities, its regulatory obligations, and long-term financial objectives. Consulting with an accountant or financial expert is suggested to find the most suitable technique for your LLC.

6.4 Which Method Do You Use?

Determining whether to utilize cash-based or accrual-based accounting mostly relies on several criteria relating to your LLC's size, business, financial demands, and regulatory requirements.

1. Choosing Between Cash and Accrual Basis Accounting:

Size of the business:

Cash Basis: More appropriate for smaller enterprises with uncomplicated transactions and less complexity.

Accrual Basis: Better for bigger organizations with considerable credit transactions and sophisticated financial procedures.

Financial reporting needs:

Cash Basis: Provides a simplified, direct snapshot of cash flow but may not present a full financial picture.

Accrual Basis: Offers a more accurate and complete perspective of the company's financial condition over time.

Regulatory Compliance:

Cash Basis: Often utilized for tax reasons by smaller enterprises owing to convenience in reporting cash transactions.

Accrual Basis: It is often necessary for bigger organizations or those that provide credit to comply with Generally Accepted Accounting Principles (GAAP) regulations.

Business Operations:

Cash Basis: Suitable for enterprises mainly dealing in cash and having few credit transactions.

Accrual Basis: More useful for organizations with substantial credit transactions, inventory management, or complicated revenue recognition.

Long-Term Planning:

monetary Basis: Might hamper long-term financial analysis owing to its immediate monetary concentration.

Accrual Basis: Provides a more accurate perspective of long-term financial patterns and performance.

Selecting the best accounting technique for your LLC entails examining the type of your firm, financial objectives, compliance needs, and the degree of financial insights required for decision-making. For a more immediate, simpler picture, cash basis could serve, but for a more thorough, accurate financial depiction, particularly for bigger or more complicated businesses, accrual basis accounting is frequently more acceptable. Consulting with an accountant or financial adviser may aid in determining the most suitable decision for your LLC's unique requirements and objectives.

6.5 How to Set Up Your Bookkeeping System

1. Do It Yourself Bookkeeping.

Setting up an accounting system for your LLC includes many phases, beginning with picking the correct solution adapted to your business's requirements. Here's a quick summary of one approach:

Choose Accounting Software:

Select accounting software that meets your company's size and needs.

Popular solutions include QuickBooks, Xero, Wave, or FreshBooks, providing varying features and functions.

Organize Financial Documents:

Gather and arrange all financial documents, such as receipts, invoices, bank statements, and spending records.

Maintain a systematic file system to readily access and save papers.

Set up a chart of accounts:

Create a chart of accounts inside your chosen accounting software, specifying numerous categories for monitoring revenue, spending, assets, and liabilities particular to your firm.

Record Transactions:

Enter all financial transactions precisely into the accounting program frequently.

Ensure transactions are classified accurately to preserve accurate financial records.

Reconcile bank statements:

Regularly reconcile bank and credit card statements with your accounting records to uncover any anomalies and assure correctness.

Generate financial reports:

Utilize the accounting software to create financial reports such as profit and loss statements, balance sheets, cash flow statements, etc., for improved insight into your LLC's financial health.

Stay updated and educated:

Keep current with accounting best practices and any changes in tax laws or regulations impacting your organization.

Consider obtaining advice from accounting resources, online tutorials, or classes to enhance your bookkeeping abilities.

Regular Reviews and Adjustments:

Review financial records frequently to discover problems or discrepancies and make required corrections.

Ensure compliance with tax filing requirements and deadlines.

DIY accounting enables hands-on administration of your LLC's financial records, allowing direct control over your company's cash.

However, it needs effort, attention to detail, and a desire to remain current with accounting standards and software functions. For complicated transactions or if time restrictions occur, getting expert accounting advice could be advantageous.

Consider the intricacy of your LLC's financial operations and your competence before selecting for DIY accounting or outsourcing the process to specialists.

1. Outsourced Bookkeeping.

Outsourcing your LLC's accounting provides various benefits, particularly if handling money isn't your forte or if you prefer to concentrate on other elements of your firm. Here's a little glance at the process:

Identify bookkeeping needs:

Assess your business's accounting requirements, including the number of transactions, complexity, and reporting demands.

Find a Reputable Service Provider:

Research and find a trusted accounting firm or professional accountant with expertise in managing LLCs and an understanding of your sector.

Share financial information:

Provide the outsourced bookkeeper with access to your financial papers, transactions, invoices, bank statements, and other essential data to maintain correct records.

Collaborate on Bookkeeping Setup:

Work with the service provider to build a simplified procedure for providing papers, documenting transactions, and getting financial data.

Regular reporting and updates:

The outsourced bookkeeper will handle your financial records, guaranteeing accuracy, reconciling accounts, and creating reports as required.

Communicate and review:

Maintain open contact with the outsourced accounting firm to review financial updates, explain any differences, and maintain compliance with tax requirements.

Maintain Oversight:

While the accounting is outsourced, retain monitoring of your financial records to ensure they correspond with your company objectives and expectations.

Regularly Assess Performance:

Evaluate the performance of the outsourced accounting service frequently to verify that it suits your business's demands successfully.

Outsourcing accounting may free up your time and give you professional experience, assuring accurate financial records and compliance with tax requirements. However, it's crucial to find a reliable service provider and maintain contact to ensure they understand your business's peculiarities and needs. Regular evaluations and monitoring help guarantee that outsourced accounting matches your LLC's aims.

1. In-House Bookkeeping

In-house accounting includes handling your LLC's financial records internally rather than outsourcing this duty to an external service provider. Here's an overview:

Establish bookkeeping procedures:

Develop consistent methods for documenting transactions, handling invoices, reconciling accounts, and creating financial reports.

Utilize accounting software:

Choose proper accounting software that corresponds with your company's demands and delivers capabilities for effective bookkeeping. Train your personnel on its utilization.

Assign Responsibilities:

Designate certain persons or a team inside your business to undertake accounting chores, guaranteeing clarity and responsibility.

Maintain accurate records:

Record all financial transactions correctly and routinely. This comprises bills, receipts, payments, costs, and other financial transactions.

Reconciliation and Reporting:

Regularly reconcile bank accounts, examine financial statements, and prepare reports (such as income statements and balance sheets) for insights into your business's financial health.

Compliance and Tax Preparation:

Ensure compliance with tax requirements by keeping correct records and producing relevant documents for tax filing purposes.

Regular Audits and Reviews:

Conduct quarterly audits or reviews of your in-house accounting systems to uncover any anomalies, verify accuracy, and maintain consistency.

Staff Training and Development:

Continuously educate and update your team on bookkeeping procedures, software upgrades, and any changes in accounting standards or legislation.

In-house accounting enables more control and quick access to financial information. However, it takes investing in software, training workers, and spending time and money to run the process properly. Regular reviews and audits assist in ensuring accuracy and compliance. It's vital to have competent people and trustworthy processes in place to maintain the integrity of your financial records.

6.6 How to Keep Track of Your Expenses

Keeping track of costs is vital for preserving the financial health of an LLC. Here's a strategy to successfully manage and track expenses:

Tracking LLC Expenses:

Categorize Expenses:

Organize costs into categories (e.g., office supplies, utilities, rent, staff wages, marketing) for easier understanding and administration.

Use Expense Tracking Tools:

Employ accounting software or specific expenditure tracking solutions that offer simple entry, classification, and tracking of all expenses.

Receipt Management:

Maintain a systematic strategy for collecting and preserving receipts or invoices. Digital tools or applications may assist in storing and managing these papers.

Regular Expense Reviews:

Schedule routine evaluations of expenditures to discover any inconsistencies, excessive costs, or areas where spending may be minimized.

Expense Reports:

Generate periodical reports detailing spending by category, department, or project. This assists in analyzing expenditure trends and budget allocation.

Budget Allocation:

Establish and routinely evaluate a budget for various expenditure categories to manage spending and guarantee financial stability.

Track employee expenses:

Implement a clear policy for employee spending and maintain a system to monitor and refund these charges quickly.

Monitor cash flow:

Analyze costs in the context of cash flow to ensure that outgoing payments line up with incoming income and do not strain the company's finances.

Expense Audits:

Conduct quarterly expenditure audits to check accuracy, identify any possible problems, and ensure compliance with corporate rules and laws.

Adaptation and Optimization:

Continuously adjust your cost monitoring techniques, tools, and procedures to enhance efficiency and accuracy.

Maintaining a thorough system to monitor spending aids in improved financial management and decision-making. It helps identify areas where expenses may be cut, guarantees compliance with tax legislation, and adds to overall financial stability and development.

Chapter Seven

Filing Taxes as an LLC

7.1 Requirements for Single-Member LLCs

Filing taxes as a single-member LLC includes unique procedures. Here's an overview of what's normally needed:

Federal Tax Filing:

File taxes as a disregarded entity by utilizing the member's tax return (Form 1040) and adding a Schedule C for business income and losses.

State Tax Filings:

Comply with state tax duties, which vary by state. Some states charge income or franchise taxes, while others may have additional obligations.

Employer Identification Number (EIN):

Obtain an EIN from the IRS if the LLC employs workers, operates as a partnership, or desires to be taxed as a corporation.

Estimated Taxes:

Pay estimated taxes quarterly to meet federal and state income tax responsibilities, similar to what a sole proprietorship would do.

Self-Employment Taxes:

Pay self-employment taxes, including Social Security and Medicare contributions, depending on the LLC's net profits.

Tax Deductions and Credits:

Take advantage of applicable tax deductions and credits to lessen the LLC's taxable income and reduce the total tax burden.

Annual Reporting:

File an annual report or statement of information, depending on the state's requirements, to maintain compliance.

Tax Year Election:

Choose a fiscal year or follow the calendar year for tax reporting, conforming to IRS laws and norms.

It's vital to be informed of tax rules and regulations related to single-member LLCs, guaranteeing compliance with federal, state, and local tax duties.

7.2 Requirements for Multiple-Member LLCs.

For a multiple-member LLC, tax regulations entail considerations beyond those of a single-member LLC. Here's an overview:

Federal Tax Filing:

File taxes as a partnership (Form 1065) by filing an informative return documenting the LLC's income, losses, deductions, and credits.

Members get a Schedule K-1, which explains each member's part of the LLC's earnings, losses, and other tax-related issues to report on their tax returns.

State Tax Filings:

Similar to single-member LLCs, they have complete state tax responsibilities, including income, franchise, or other taxes as per the state's laws.

Employer Identification Number (EIN):

Obtain an EIN if the LLC has workers or if it elects to be taxed as a corporation.

Estimated Taxes:

Make quarterly anticipated tax payments to meet federal and state income tax responsibilities for each member's portion.

Self-Employment Taxes:

Members may owe self-employment taxes on their part of the LLC's income, paying Social Security and Medicare taxes on their earnings.

Tax Deductions and Credits:

Utilize applicable tax deductions and credits to lower the LLC's taxable revenue, affecting each member's tax responsibility.

Annual Reporting:

File a yearly informative return with the IRS, including facts on the LLC's financial activities and distribution among members.

Operating Agreement and Tax Matters:

The operational agreement describes how revenues and losses are allocated among members, affecting each member's tax responsibility.

Understanding and complying with these tax regulations are critical for multiple-member LLCs to maintain compliance and manage their tax responsibilities efficiently. Would you need further information on any particular component of tax filing for multiple-member LLCs or go with the next section?

7.3 C-Corp Versus S-Corp

1. C-Corporation (C-Corp)

Tax Structure:

C-Corps are independent tax entities from their owners.

Subject to corporate income tax on earnings, shareholders are taxed separately on dividends paid.

Tax Filing:

File Form 1120 to record income, deductions, profits, losses, and other business financial information.

Profits are taxed at the corporate level, while dividends issued to shareholders are taxed again on their tax returns (double taxation).

Ownership and Structure:

There are no limits on the number of stockholders or their residency.

Offers flexibility in issuing numerous classes of stock.

Maintains a formal organization with directors, officers, and stockholders.

Shareholders and Liability:

There is limited responsibility for shareholders, meaning their assets are often safeguarded from business debts and obligations.

Can attract external investment via the sale of shares.

Regulatory Compliance:

Compliance with significant regulatory and governance standards.

Required to convene regular shareholder and board of director meetings and keep accurate corporate records.

Benefits:

Easier access to finance via the selling of stocks.

Potential for corporate development and growth.

Can give stock options and other rewards to workers.

C-Corporations are appropriate for organizations looking to develop, obtain funds via investors, or ultimately go public. However, the double taxation aspect might be a problem for certain firms.

Would you want to examine the characteristics and contrasts of an S-Corporation compared to a C-Corporation, or go further into any single area of C-Corps?

1. S-Corporation (S-Corp)

Tax Structure:

travel-through taxes: Profits and losses travel through the business to shareholders' tax returns, avoiding double taxation.

There is no federal income tax at the business level; instead, shareholders record their share of earnings and losses on individual tax forms.

Tax Filing:

File Form 1120S to record income, deductions, profits, losses, and other firm financial information.

Profits and losses are apportioned to shareholders according to their ownership percentages.

Ownership and Structure:

Limited to 100 stockholders or less, who must be U.S. citizens or residents.

Can issue just one class of stock.

Operates with a formal organization comprising directors, officials, and stockholders.

Shareholders and Liability:

Offers limited liability protection to shareholders against corporate debts and liabilities.

Can attract investment via the sale of shares, but with limits owing to the cap on the number of shareholders.

Regulatory Compliance:

Similar to C-corporations, S-corporations have compliance standards but often have less formality and governance duties.

Benefits:

Avoids double taxation since earnings pass through to shareholders' tax returns.

Provides limited responsibility to stockholders.

Can give some tax benefits to shareholders.

S-corporations are suited for small to medium-sized firms looking to avoid double taxation while keeping some of the benefits of a corporation form. However, the qualifying requirements and constraints on ownership make it less flexible for bigger enterprises.

7.4 Estimated Tax, What and Why?

Estimated tax refers to periodic tax payments made by individuals and organizations, including LLCs, on income that is not subject to withholding tax. It's simply a strategy to avoid tax underpayment throughout the year. These payments generally include income tax, self-employment tax, and alternative minimum tax (AMT).

For an LLC, projected tax payments can be required if the firm anticipates owing at least $1,000 in taxes when its return is submitted. If the LLC's revenue isn't subject to withholding, such as profits from self-employment, interest, dividends, rent, or alimony, it's best to estimate and pay taxes quarterly. These payments often fall at specified times throughout the year.

The goal of anticipated taxes is to avert a big tax bill at the end of the year and to assure a consistent flow of tax income to the government. By making frequent anticipated tax payments, LLCs avoid fines and interest costs for underpayment.

Estimated tax calculations entail calculating yearly income, deductions, credits, and tax rates. It's crucial to precisely anticipate revenue to prevent overpayment or underpayment, both of which might have financial ramifications for the LLC.

Businesses may utilize IRS Form 1040-ES to compute and pay estimated taxes. These payments are paid quarterly, generally due on April 15th, June 15th, September 15th, and January 15th of the following year. However, dates could change if they occur on weekends or holidays.

Remember, this procedure may be difficult, and receiving help from an accountant or tax specialist is generally advised to guarantee compliance and precise computations.

7.5 How to Calculate the Estimated Tax.

Calculating estimated taxes entails predicting income and deductions to establish the tax due for the year. For an LLC, calculating taxes may be done utilizing multiple income sources, including fixed revenue, variable income, fixed expenditures, variable expenses, and a personal tax component.

1. Fixed Income

Identify Fixed Income Sources: Include earnings from regular sources such as wages, rentals, royalties, or other guaranteed income.

Determine Gross Revenue: Add together all fixed revenue sources to determine the total gross income.

Consider Deductions: Deduct eligible business expenditures, permitted deductions, or credits from the gross income to arrive at the taxable income.

Apply Tax Rates: Calculate the expected tax based on the taxable income and the relevant tax rates for the LLC's classification (such as a single-member LLC or partnership).

Estimated taxes for fixed income sources could be easier to forecast since they stay generally steady throughout the year. However, it's vital to keep track of any changes or variations in these sources to update tax calculations appropriately.

Consulting a tax expert or utilizing tax software helps speed this procedure and ensure proper computations. Remember, underestimating taxes may result in fines, so it's essential to frequently examine and revise your projected tax payments.

1. Variable Income

Variable income, unlike fixed income, varies and could provide issues in determining tax requirements. For an LLC, this form of revenue may include irregular profits from investments, contracts, or sales commissions, among others.

Estimating Variable Income Tax:

Track revenue Sources: Maintain thorough records of changeable revenue sources. This includes invoices, contracts, sales records, or other documents showing future profits.

Forecast Future profits: Use historical records and expected income to forecast probable future profits.

Anticipate swings: Account for probable swings in variable revenue by examining seasonal variations, market trends, or changes in customers or contracts.

Calculate Taxes: Once the possible variable income is estimated, apply the applicable tax rates to determine the tax bill.

Given the variety, it's recommended to revisit these estimations often, particularly if the business environment changes or new revenue sources arise. Setting aside a percentage of variable income for taxes might help lessen any unexpected tax bills at year-end. Consulting a tax professional or utilizing financial software that aids in tax calculation based on fluctuating income may give better precision.

1. Fixed Expenses

Estimating expected taxes by considering fixed expenditures includes analyzing the constant costs your LLC incurs throughout the year. These costs often stay consistent or have a known pattern, making it easy to determine tax consequences.

Steps to Estimate Tax Based on Fixed Expenses:

Identify Fixed Expenses: List any recurrent expenditures needed to run your LLC, such as rent, utilities, insurance fees, wages, and depreciation.

Calculate Total Fixed charges: Sum together all these charges to obtain the total fixed expenses incurred by the LLC.

Deduct Fixed expenditures from gross income: Subtract the total fixed expenditures from the gross income (revenue minus fixed expenses) to get the taxable income.

Apply Tax Rates: Calculate the expected tax due based on the taxable revenue using the applicable tax rates for your LLC.

Understanding and effectively accounting for fixed costs assists in estimating the LLC's tax requirements. However, note that certain fixed costs may be deductible or subject to particular tax treatment, so consultation with a tax expert is essential for clarity and maximizing tax benefits. Regularly monitoring and updating these projections is critical, particularly if any fixed costs alter over the year.

1. Variable Expenses

Variable expenditures in an LLC, unlike fixed expenses, change depending on company activity, sales volume, or operational demands. These costs could include supplies, utilities, commissions, or marketing charges that fluctuate depending on the degree of company activity.

Estimating Tax Based on Variable Expenses:

Track Variable Costs: Maintain records of all variable expenditures incurred throughout company operations.

Assess Past Expenses: Review historical data to determine trends or averages for these variable expenditures throughout various periods.

Forecast Future expenditures: Use past data to forecast projected variable expenditures based on anticipated company activities or growth.

Deduct Variable expenditures from Revenue: Subtract the estimated variable expenditures from the LLC's revenue to get the taxable income.

Apply Tax Rates: Calculate the expected tax due based on the taxable income using the appropriate tax rates.

Regularly assessing and revising these projections is critical, particularly if there are substantial changes in company operations or cost trends. Seeking counsel from a tax expert helps enable more precise calculations and helps leverage possible tax savings connected to variable costs.

1. Personal Tax Component

The personal tax component applies to the tax responsibilities of the LLC's members. In a pass-through business like an LLC, income and losses flow through to the individual members' tax returns, and they are responsible for reporting these items on their tax files.

Understanding the Personal Tax Component:

Pass-Through Taxation: In a single-member LLC, the owner discloses company income and losses on their tax return using Schedule C of Form 1040. For multi-member LLCs, each member gets a Schedule K-1, reflecting their portion of earnings or losses, which they disclose on their tax returns.

Taxable Income from LLC: Members pay taxes on their part of the LLC's earnings, whether or not these gains are dispersed. Losses might also counterbalance other income the members have.

Self-Employment Tax: Members who are engaged in the LLC's activities may owe self-employment taxes on their share of earnings, covering Medicare and Social Security.

Estimated Tax Payments: Members would need to make quarterly estimated tax payments to meet their tax responsibilities arising from the LLC's income.

Understanding the personal tax ramifications is crucial for LLC members. They should engage closely with tax consultants or accountants to guarantee correct reporting, compliance, and maximizing tax strategies about their unique tax circumstances.

CHAPTER EIGHT

DISSOLVING AN LLC.

8.1 When Should You Dissolve Your LLC?

1. If the Purpose for Creating the LLC Has Been fulfilled or come to an End

Deciding to dissolve an LLC is a vital step that correlates with the completion or expiration of its stated purpose. If the initial purpose for founding the LLC, such as a particular project, enterprise, or commercial aim, has been completed or is no longer relevant, it could be time to contemplate dissolution. This coincides with the essential essence of an LLC: to serve a stated purpose, whether it's a short-term initiative or a long-term economic enterprise.

Continuing to maintain an LLC without a clear, relevant purpose might lead to problems. Therefore, examining whether the LLC's initial goals have been realized or have become outdated is vital. This examination ensures that resources, efforts, and legal duties linked with the LLC are not unduly perpetuated or maintained when they no longer serve a relevant purpose.

Additionally, if the LLC was founded for a set time or for a particular purpose that has ended, dissolution may be acceptable. This enables the official termination of the corporate entity and the fulfillment of legal duties, including tax filings and debts, to prevent unwanted continuing responsibility.

Understanding the original aim behind founding the LLC and deciding whether that purpose has been accomplished or become irrelevant serves as a vital signal for contemplating dissolution. It's a deliberate decision to appropriately finish the entity's activities in conformity with its original aims.

1. If Financial Viability No Longer Exists.

The financial health of an LLC is a significant component in determining its sustainability. When the entity suffers ongoing financial issues that restrict its capacity to function efficiently or meet its responsibilities, contemplating dissolution becomes important.

Financial viability involves numerous characteristics, including revenue creation, profitability, cash flow, and the capacity to make financial obligations such as loan payments, employee wages, operating expenditures, and taxes. If the LLC experiences continuous financial challenges that cannot be handled via regular company activities, it can signify the necessity for dissolution.

Chronic financial instability may come from several reasons, such as diminishing revenue, excessive debt, unsustainable spending, or economic downturns impacting the business. If attempts to solve these financial challenges—through restructuring, cost-cutting measures, seeking more capital, or diversifying income streams—prove ineffective, the sustainability of the LLC could be in peril.

Continuing operations under such conditions might lead to bankruptcy, creditor proceedings, or legal issues. Dissolution could be the wisest course of action to reduce future financial losses, safeguard stakeholders, and prevent personal culpability for the LLC's obligations.

In such instances, dissolution provides for an orderly completion of the LLC's business, including collecting outstanding debts, completing contractual obligations, and correctly dividing leftover assets among members or stakeholders. It's a responsible action to limit financial risks and avoid unfavorable outcomes that might harm both the organization and the persons affiliated with it.

Overall, recognizing the lack of financial viability as a compelling ground for dissolution is a deliberate decision to safeguard the interests of the LLC, its members, and other stakeholders from any financial loss or legal ramifications coming from unsustainable financial circumstances.

8.2 Types of Dissolution.

1. Voluntary Dissolution

Voluntary dissolution stands as a conscious choice by the LLC members to discontinue the company's activities and formally disband the firm. This dissolution type happens in many situations, mainly when the members determine that continued activities are no longer viable or desirable.

One significant cause for voluntary dissolution might be the attainment of the LLC's purpose or the awareness that the business objectives have been met. For instance, a project-based LLC, founded to execute a particular work or enterprise, can decide for voluntary dissolution after completing its mission. Additionally, LLCs created for a certain time or to implement a specific business plan could voluntarily dissolve after that term ends or the strategy becomes outmoded.

Another situation causing voluntary dissolution is members' consent to end the firm owing to irreconcilable disputes or conflicts among them. In circumstances when the members' relationship deteriorates to a degree that continuous cooperation is impossible or destructive to the firm, they could select voluntary dissolution as an amicable approach to dissolve the corporation and move ahead independently. Financial bankruptcy or the inability to continue operations owing to insurmountable financial issues may also induce voluntary dissolution. When the LLC suffers serious debt, lack of cash to meet operating expenditures, or chronic financial losses that cannot be addressed, members may decide on voluntary dissolution to reduce additional financial risks and responsibilities.

Moreover, some LLCs could contemplate voluntary dissolution if the business climate suddenly changes, making their activities unviable or irrelevant. This might include changes in market circumstances, industry disruptions, or legislative revisions that substantially influence the business model or the market demand for the LLC's goods or services.

Examples of voluntary dissolution circumstances might include project-based LLCs founded to produce a particular product. Once the product is successfully released or the project is done, the LLC could dissolve. Similarly, if a group of people joins together to operate a seasonal company, such as a pop-up shop during the Christmas season, they could dissolve the LLC after the season finishes.

Voluntary dissolution is started by the LLC members following the method established in the state's LLC legislation. This normally requires conducting a meeting among the members, writing and passing a resolution to dissolve the LLC, contacting creditors and paying obligations, and completing appropriate documentation to file for dissolution with the state authorities.

Ultimately, voluntary dissolution reflects an intentional and agreed-upon choice by the LLC members to stop the company's activities and perform the requisite legal requirements to finish the entity's existence in a way that complies with the state laws and regulations regulating LLC dissolution.

1. Involuntary Dissolution

Involuntary dissolution of an LLC happens when external forces or legal bodies compel the suspension of company activities against the wishes of the members. Unlike voluntary dissolution, when the decision arises from the members' choice, forced dissolution is often precipitated by external reasons such as court decisions, regulatory activities, or legal obligations.

Several causes might lead to an involuntary dissolution. One typical reason is the inability to comply with state rules or statutory requirements, such as failing to submit essential reports, pay taxes, or retain a registered agent. If an LLC persistently neglects its legal commitments, the state regulatory authority could commence involuntary dissolution procedures against the company.

Similarly, an LLC may suffer forced dissolution owing to court orders stemming from legal disputes among members or with other parties. In circumstances of unresolved internal disagreements or extended disputes among members, a court might mandate the dissolution of the corporation as a settlement to the deadlock. This situation commonly emerges when the LLC's activities are inhibited by continual arguments among members, making it impractical to continue doing business.

Furthermore, if an LLC participates in fraudulent activities, acts illegally, or breaches its operating agreement in a way that causes severe injury or violates public policy, a judge may compel its involuntary dissolution. Fraudulent acts, misrepresentation, or unlawful operations might cause legal measures leading to the dissolution of the LLC to safeguard the interests of stakeholders and the public.

Additionally, an LLC might suffer forced dissolution owing to its inability to satisfy specified contractual responsibilities, such as obligations towards creditors or partners. If an LLC regularly breaks contractual agreements or fails to satisfy its financial responsibilities despite warnings or letters from creditors or partners, it could face legal measures that culminate in forced dissolution.

Involuntary dissolution frequently entails legal actions launched by interested parties or regulatory organizations via a petition or lawsuit filed in the proper court. The court assesses the facts, examines the evidence given, and, if the reasons for dissolution are legitimate, gives a decision for the dissolution of the LLC.

Instances of forced dissolution can include circumstances when an LLC routinely fails to complete necessary yearly reports or tax returns despite repeated warnings from the state's secretary of state. Another scenario might be an LLC engaging in fraudulent operations, resulting in legal proceedings from impacted parties or regulatory bodies and dissolution.

In summary, involuntary dissolution indicates the end of an LLC's operations owing to external reasons, legal proceedings, or court orders that force the suspension of commercial activity against the desire of the LLC members.

CONCLUSION

The process of founding, operating, and dissolving an LLC includes various factors and choices that greatly affect the performance and sustainability of the company entity. From grasping the foundations of what an LLC comprises to appreciating the subtleties of picking the correct structure, completing essential paperwork, and adhering to legal and financial duties, the path of an LLC owner is diverse and demands intelligent decision-making.

Starting with the birth of the concept of forming an LLC, it's vital to comprehend the core of what it means to be part of a limited liability company. Understanding the benefits, such as liability protection and flexible taxes, and the downsides, including administrative needs and possible constraints, is crucial in making an educated selection. Additionally, digging into the subtleties of single- and multiple-member LLCs and the numerous sorts of LLC structures assures alignment with the business's goals.

The process of creating an LLC comprises a methodical set of stages, from picking an appropriate name to completing important papers and getting relevant permits. Each phase involves rigorous attention to detail and compliance with state rules to ensure a flawless and legally sound setup. Throughout the LLC's lifecycle, avoiding frequent hazards and blunders becomes vital. Missteps in company selection, regulatory concerns, poor paperwork, or combining personal and corporate money may pose major dangers. Properly addressing these possible problems and maintaining solid operating agreements and precise record-keeping processes are crucial to preserving the LLC's stability and development.

Moreover, examining the possibilities of converting an existing firm into an LLC, knowing the accounting and taxation factors, and appreciating the ramifications of paying taxes as an LLC are key components of effective LLC administration.

Lastly, identifying when it may be time to dissolve the LLC, knowing the reasons and processes for dissolution, and grasping the repercussions of involuntary dissolution help LLC owners make educated choices while safeguarding their interests and complying with legal duties.

In summary, the path of operating an LLC is a dynamic and developing process that involves ongoing learning, flexibility, and adherence to legal and operational best practices. While there are various hurdles and complexity involved, a well-informed and proactive strategy may pave the way for a successful and sustained LLC enterprise.

S CORPORATION BEGINNER'S GUIDE

Reid C. Williams
THE ULTIMATE LLC AND S-CORPORATION BEGINNER'S GUIDE

INTRODUCTION

S companies, commonly known as S corps, constitute a distinct corporate type within the commercial environment. Their structure provides various benefits and considerations for individuals seeking a company structure with particular tax advantages. An S corporation is not a commercial entity itself but rather a tax classification provided by the IRS to qualified firms.

Eligibility conditions for a S company are particular. The company must be a domestic business, have only allowed shareholders, including persons, certain trusts, and estates, and not exceed a limited number of shareholders (currently fixed at 100 individuals).

Why go for an S company over a C corporation? One significant factor is the tax treatment. Unlike a regular C corporation, where the organization pays taxes on its revenue and shareholders pay taxes on dividends received, a S corporation's earnings and losses "pass through" directly to shareholders' tax returns. This eliminates the double taxes inherent with C companies.

Benefits of a S company include pass-through taxes, restricted responsibility for shareholders, possible tax savings, and the possibility to recruit investors by giving stock ownership. However, these advantages come with significant limits. For instance, S companies cannot have more than 100 stockholders and must be held by U.S. citizens or resident aliens.

Comparing S corporations to LLCs highlights variations in structure, tax treatment, and ownership limits. While both companies provide limited liability protection, LLCs allow for greater flexibility in terms of ownership, taxes, and operating structures compared to S corporations.

Understanding the nuances of forming, administering, and negotiating the tax issues of an S company is vital for business owners. In the coming sections, we'll look more into eligibility criteria, the process of creating an S corporation, the duties and obligations of stakeholders, tax consequences, conversion from other company structures, traps to avoid, and the dissolution procedure.

Are you ready to study the subtleties of S companies and their repercussions further?

Reid C. Williams

THE ULTIMATE LLC AND S-CORPORATION BEGINNER'S GUIDE

CHAPTER 1

WHAT IS AN S CORPORATION?

1.1. Definition of an S company

An S company, sometimes referred to as an S corp, is a separate tax status issued by the IRS to qualified small enterprises. Unlike a separate corporate structure, it's not a business entity but rather a tax categorization that firms may designate for special tax treatment.

An S company provides a unique mix of partnership and corporate qualities. It permits the firm to avoid the double taxes experienced by regular C companies. Instead of paying corporate income taxes, S companies transmit their revenue, deductions, losses, and credits to their owners, who record them on their tax forms.

To qualify for S-company status, certain qualifying conditions must be met. The company must be a domestic business (working in the United States), have no more than 100 shareholders, only contain eligible shareholders (individuals, certain trusts, and estates), and maintain only one class of stock.

This categorization enables company owners to benefit from the restricted liability of a corporation while enjoying pass-through tax benefits comparable to those of partnerships or sole proprietorships. The notion of S companies was created to offer smaller firms the advantages of incorporation while avoiding some of the taxation issues experienced by larger organizations. Understanding the intricacies of how an S company functions and its tax ramifications is vital for entrepreneurs contemplating this organizational form.

1.2. What makes it an S corporation?

An S company, called after subsection S of the Internal Revenue Code, gets its status by completing specific conditions and filing an election with the IRS. What classifies it as a S corp are many crucial characteristics:

Pass-through Taxation: One of the distinguishing aspects of an S company is its pass-through taxes. Profits and losses are not taxed at the corporate level; instead, they "pass-through" to the shareholders' tax returns, where they are recorded and taxed appropriately. This form helps prevent double taxation, a major problem encountered by C businesses.

Limited Liability Protection: Similar to C companies, S corporations give limited liability protection to their stockholders. Shareholders are not individually accountable for the company's debts and legal responsibilities. Their liability is normally restricted to the amount of their investment in the firm.

Ownership and Shareholders: S companies have special constraints on ownership. They cannot have more than 100 shareholders, and all stockholders must be U.S. citizens or residents, specified trusts, or estates. Additionally, S companies may only issue one class of shares.

IRS Election: To become an S corporation, a firm must submit Form 2553 with the IRS and fulfill certain eligibility conditions, such as having a domestic business structure, keeping eligible stockholders, and meeting stock ownership restrictions.

Business Structure and Operations: S companies must conform to certain corporate formalities, such as having regular shareholder and director meetings, preserving minutes, and maintaining separate financial records.

These criteria jointly describe what characterizes an S company. Understanding these contrasts is crucial for company owners contemplating this organization form, as it provides a mix of liability protection and tax benefits that suit specific kinds of small to medium-sized firms.

1.3. Why decide on an S-corp?

Selecting a S-company form generally derives from its distinct benefits, appealing notably to small and mid-sized firms. Here are convincing reasons why businesses could choose an S corporation:

flow-through taxation: S companies avoid double taxation, enabling income and losses to flow through to shareholders' tax returns. This feature permits business income to be taxed at individual rates rather than corporate rates, possibly resulting in tax savings.

Limited Liability: Similar to other corporate arrangements, an S corporation offers limited liability protection, insulating owners' assets from the company's responsibilities and debts.

Tax Flexibility: Shareholders of S companies may receive both salaries and payouts. While wages are subject to payroll taxes, distributions may be taxed at a reduced rate, creating possible tax-saving options for shareholders.

Ease of Raising Funds: S companies may attract investors by issuing shares of stock, allowing for the injection of funds into the firm via share sales.

Credibility and Perpetuity: Operating as a S company may boost credibility with consumers, suppliers, and partners. Additionally, this firm form promotes continuity and durability since ownership may be transferred relatively readily via the sale of shares.

Retirement Benefits: S company owners might potentially benefit from retirement plans, including contributions to SEP IRAs, 401(k)s, and other retirement accounts, providing for tax-deferred savings.

Legal Protection: The structure offers a layer of legal protection, reducing the personal responsibility of shareholders against corporate debts and legal responsibilities.

The choice to pick an S company should coincide with the unique objectives, aims, and nature of the firm. While these benefits are attractive, it's vital to evaluate qualifying criteria, compliance requirements, and the business's long-term goals before making the choice. Consulting with legal and financial consultants may give useful insights into whether an S company is the most suitable solution for a specific firm.

1.4. Benefits and Drawbacks of a S Corporation

S companies come with a range of benefits and drawbacks:

Benefits:

flow-through taxation: The trademark characteristic of S companies is that income and losses flow through to shareholders' tax returns, eliminating double taxation.

Limited Liability: Shareholders receive limited liability protection, insulating their assets from the company's debts or legal proceedings.

Tax Flexibility: Shareholders may receive dividends and salaries, possibly decreasing their total tax obligation by getting distributions taxed at a lower rate than wages.

Attractiveness to Investors: The ability to issue shares may tempt investors and allow cash injections into the organization.

Perpetual Existence: S companies may exist even if shareholders alter or transfer their ownership.

Drawbacks:

Eligibility Requirements: S companies have tight qualifying restrictions, including constraints on the number and kind of shareholders, which could restrict expansion potential.

Tax Complexity: Though pass-through taxes are favorable, they may lead to complications in tax forms, requiring rigorous accounting and tax compliance.

Limited Growth Potential: The structure might be constraining for firms wanting to develop by recruiting new investors since the number of shareholders is restricted.

severe Operational Rules: S companies must conform to more formalities than other company kinds, requiring frequent shareholder meetings and severe record-keeping.

Eligibility Restrictions: Non-U.S. residents, certain trusts, and other companies cannot be shareholders, placing constraints on ownership.

While the rewards are enticing, the constraints and complications demand careful thought. For firms striving for development and flexibility while keeping minimal responsibility, an S company might be helpful. However, it's crucial to consider the trade-offs against the unique demands and future ambitions of the organization before picking this structure. Consulting with legal and financial specialists is vital to making an educated choice.

1.5. Comparing S Corporation Vs LLC: Differences and Benefits

Certainly, comparing a S Corporation (S Corp) with a Limited Liability Company (LLC) includes assessing their distinctions and relative benefits.

1. Structural Differences:

Ownership: S Corps is restricted to 100 shareholders, but LLCs may have an unlimited number of members.

Ownership Restrictions: S Corps have severe ownership rules, permitting only U.S. citizens and residents as stockholders, whereas LLCs have greater freedom in ownership.

Management: S Corps have a stronger management structure with specified executives and a board of directors, whereas LLCs may be more flexible in their administration and organization.

Formalities: S Corps often have greater formalities, such as mandated yearly meetings and thorough record-keeping, compared to the more flexible operating needs of LLCs.

1. taxes: tax treatment:

S Corps and LLCs both receive pass-through taxes, meaning income is passed through to shareholders or members, avoiding double taxation at the corporate level.

Self-Employment Tax: S Corp. stockholders who actively engage in the firm may be obliged to pay self-employment tax on their salaries but not on payouts. In contrast, LLC members normally pay self-employment tax on their entire income.

Flexibility: S Corps provides more specified means for dividing earnings, while LLCs allow greater flexibility in profit distribution among members.

1. Credibility and Perceptions:

Credibility: S Corps frequently has a more established and recognized corporate structure, which may be useful when working with investors, lenders, or partners.

Perception: Some sectors or stakeholders may regard S Corps as more official and organized compared to LLCs, impacting business relationships or contracts.

1. Legal Protection:

Limited Liability: Both corporations give limited liability protection to their shareholders and members, safeguarding personal assets from business responsibilities.

Operational Formalities: Maintaining these safeguards typically involves rigorous attention to operational formalities for both S Corps and LLCs.

1. Operational Requirements:

freedom: LLCs often have greater freedom in management, operational organization, and ownership compared to S Corps, which have more regulated governance.

Record-keeping: S Corps sometimes have more severe record-keeping obligations compared to LLCs, demanding extensive meeting minutes and financial documents.

Choosing Between the Two:

The decision between an S Corp. and an LLC generally relies on the unique demands of the firm, its long-term objectives, the intended structure of ownership and management, tax concerns, and the industry's expectations or preferences. Consulting legal, financial, or tax specialists may assist in making an educated choice customized to the business's particular circumstances.

CHAPTER 2

ESTABLISHING AN S CORPORATION

2.1 Eligibility criteria for S corporations

Eligibility requirements for S companies are high and must be satisfied to qualify for this tax status. Primarily, a S company must be a domestic organization, established inside the United States, and satisfy particular guidelines:

Limited Shareholders: S companies are confined to 100 shareholders or less. These shareholders may be people, certain trusts, or estates, but not partnerships, corporations, or non-resident alien shareholders.

Eligible Shareholders: Shareholders must be U.S. citizens or residents, certain trusts, and tax-exempt organizations, excluding partnerships, corporations, and non-resident alien shareholders.

One Class of Stock: An S company may issue just one class of stock. This implies all shareholders must have the same rights concerning dividends, distributions, and liquidation profits.

Business Type Restriction: Certain kinds of firms are ineligible for S-corporation status, including certain banking institutions, insurance companies, and foreign sales corporations.

Tax Year Reporting: S companies follow a calendar year unless they have a compelling business justification to adopt a fiscal year.

Submission of Form 2553: To elect S corporation status, a company must submit Form 2553, Election by a Small Business Corporation, with the IRS within a set date.

Meeting these qualifying requirements is vital for a firm wanting to establish itself as an S corporation to take advantage of its advantageous tax treatment and operational structure. It's vital to engage legal and tax specialists to assure compliance and fitness for the S company election.

2.2 Choosing a name for Your Company

Selecting a name for an S company includes adhering to specified requirements and ensuring the name matches legal and branding considerations.

Compliance: The selected name must comply with state rules. Generally, it should not be the same or too similar to existing business organizations registered in the state. Conduct a comprehensive search on the Secretary of State's website or other corporate entity databases to check name availability.

Availability: Ensure that the chosen name is available as a domain for a website and on social media networks. Consistency in the name across numerous internet platforms is crucial for branding and marketing objectives.

Distinctiveness: The name should be unique, memorable, and representative of the business's character or ideals. Avoid generic or excessively popular names to stand out in the market.

Legal Requirements: "corp. Some states can need particular phrases like "Corporation," "Corp.," or "incorporated" to be part of the firm name to designate it as a corporation.

Trademark Consideration: Check for existing trademarks to confirm the name is not already trademarked by another business. Trademark infringement might lead to legal troubles.

Reserve the Name: If the chosen name is available, several jurisdictions enable firms to reserve it for a certain period before legally forming the organization.

Careful deliberation and careful study are necessary when picking a name for a S business. It's recommended to get legal counsel or employ professional services to guarantee compliance with all legal and branding elements.

2.3 Drafting articles of incorporation for S. company

Drafting articles of incorporation for an S company includes developing a formal document that provides crucial data about the business organization. Here are the major stages in the process:

Basic Information: Start by supplying key facts such as the corporation's name, major place of business, purpose, term (if applicable), and the registered agent's name and address.

Stock Information: Specify the number of shares the company is permitted to issue, their classes (if numerous), and the par value (if any).

Directors and Officers: Outline the names and addresses of the original directors. Some states can necessitate listing officials as well.

S Corporation Election: Include a statement announcing the corporation's desire to be taxed as an S corporation. This choice lets the corporation transfer corporate income, losses, deductions, and credits through to its shareholders for federal tax purposes.

Registered Agent: Designate a registered agent who will receive legal paperwork on behalf of the company.

Filing and Fees: Once the articles are prepared, submit them to the Secretary of State or the applicable state office. Be prepared to pay the applicable filing costs.

Publication Requirements: Some states could demand extra processes, such as posting a notice of intent to incorporate a company in local newspapers.

Operating Agreement: While not essential for filing articles of incorporation, having an operating agreement that specifies how the organization will be controlled and managed and its activities performed may be extremely useful. This agreement is vital, particularly for multi-member S-companies.

Remember, articles of incorporation requirements may vary by state, so it's vital to check the precise rules issued by the state's Secretary of State or equivalent regulating body to ensure compliance with all legal duties. Consulting with a legal practitioner or a company attorney might give useful insight during this process.

2.4 Filing with the appropriate state agency

After preparing the articles of incorporation, the next step is submitting them to the proper state agency, often the Secretary of State's office or the Corporations Division. Here's an overview of the process:

Review Requirements: Before submission, check the state's unique criteria for submitting articles of incorporation. Each state has its own paperwork, fees, and processes.

Complete Forms: Fill out the essential fields properly. Include all relevant information, such as the company's name, purpose, registered agent details, incorporators' names and addresses, and the S corporation election.

Filing Fee: Prepare the filing fee according to the state's rules. The cost varies by state and may vary from a modest sum to several hundred dollars.

Submit Documents: Submit the completed articles of incorporation, together with the filing fee, to the authorized state agency. Some states may enable online filing, while others may require mailing or presenting the paperwork in person.

Confirmation and Processing: After submission, the state agency will evaluate the papers. If everything is in line, they'll process the articles of incorporation. This procedure's time varies by state but normally takes a few weeks.

Receive Confirmation: Once completed, you'll receive confirmation of the successful file. This confirmation could contain a stamped copy of the filed articles or a certificate of incorporation.

Remember, adhering to state requirements and correctly supplying all relevant information is vital for a successful filing. It's essential to preserve copies of all submitted papers and communications for your records.

Consulting with a company attorney or a specialist specializing in corporate filings may give you useful direction throughout the filing process, assuring compliance with all legal requirements and processes relevant to your state.

2.5 Obtaining an Employer Identification Number

Obtaining an employer identification number (EIN) is a vital step for a S company, just like any commercial organization. Here's a summary of the process:

EIN Application: You may apply for an EIN from the Internal Revenue Service (IRS) via different channels. The most frequent approach is filling out Form SS-4 either online, via mail, fax, or by phone.

Online Application: Applying online via the IRS website is the fastest approach. The application is uncomplicated and often produces a quick EIN upon completion.

By Mail or Fax: If applying by mail or fax, get Form SS-4 from the IRS website, fill it out with appropriate facts about your company, and then send it via the specified channels.

Phone Application: You may also acquire an EIN by calling the IRS Business and Specialty Tax Line. This technique is excellent if you prefer a phone call to deliver the relevant information.

Required Information: When applying for an EIN, you'll need facts such as the legal name and address of the S corporation, the responsible party's Social Security Number (SSN), company structure, purpose for filing, and more.

Immediate EIN Assignment: Generally, following completion of the online application, the IRS quickly supplies you with an EIN, although mail or fax applications may take a few weeks.

Record-keeping: Once you have your EIN, ensure to keep it secure and fully recorded. The EIN is utilized for many tax and business reasons, such as filing taxes, creating a company bank account, recruiting staff, and more.

Acquiring an EIN is a key step that helps identify your S company for federal tax reasons and is typically essential for numerous commercial activities and compliance needs. Always confirm the correctness of the information supplied in the application to prevent any complications in the future.

2.6 Electing S company status with the IRS.

Electing S corporation status with the IRS is vital for some firms looking to profit from this unique tax structure. Here's a summary of the process:

Eligibility: To qualify for S corporation status, your firm must fulfill specified requirements imposed by the IRS. This includes having less than 100 shareholders, being a domestic business, and having shareholders who are people, certain trusts, or estates.

Filing Form 2553: The election to become an S corporation is accomplished by submitting Form 2553, Election by a Small Business Corporation, with the IRS. This form must be submitted within a particular period, often within two and a half months after the start of the tax year the election is to take effect, or at any point during the tax year before the tax year it is to take effect.

Unanimous Shareholder Assent: In most situations, all shareholders must assent to the S company election. Exceptions exist for some eligible trusts and estates.

IRS Approval: Once Form 2553 is completed correctly and submitted to the IRS, they evaluate the application. If everything corresponds with the qualifying requirements and the paperwork is filled out, the IRS normally authorizes the S company election.

Effective Date: The election's effective date is mentioned on Form 2553. It's vital to verify that all shareholders and the company agree on the designated effective date for the S corporation classification.

Tax Treatment: Upon approval, the S company will enjoy a different tax treatment. It avoids double taxation since the corporation's revenue is often not taxed at the corporate level; instead, it goes through to shareholders, who report it on their tax forms.

Ongoing Compliance: Once the S corporation election is in place, the firm must comply with all IRS requirements for S companies, including yearly filings, satisfying shareholder and ownership requirements, and following special operating and tax laws.

Filing for S corporation status includes certain processes and regulations, and it's important to contact a tax expert or attorney to ensure correct adherence to IRS standards and optimize the advantages associated with this tax structure.

CHAPTER 3

MANAGING AN S CORPORATION

3.1 The Roles and Responsibilities of Shareholders, Directors, And Officers

1. Shareholders

Within an S corporation, stockholders occupy a key role as the owners of the firm. Their primary roles include:

Ownership: Shareholders participate in the corporation by owning shares, and their ownership determines their rights in decision-making, profits, and voting on major corporate concerns.

Voting Rights: Shareholders generally have voting rights depending on their shares, enabling them to engage in decisions affecting the business. Major decisions, such as choosing the board of directors or making substantial changes, sometimes need shareholder votes.

Profit Distribution: Shareholders are entitled to receive dividends or distributions from the company's earnings depending on their ownership percentage.

Limited Liability: They profit from limited liability, meaning their assets are safeguarded from the corporation's responsibilities, debts, or legal proceedings.

Participation in Meetings: Shareholders are invited to attend annual meetings and may participate in debates and decisions affecting the company.

Approving Major Changes: Some substantial changes, including mergers, need shareholder approval.

Understanding their rights and obligations, shareholders actively participate in the corporation's development, monitor critical decisions, and match their interests with the company's success.

1. Directors

Directors within a S-company occupy a vital role in managing business activities and making strategic choices. Their roles encompass:

Governance: Directors are chosen by shareholders and are responsible for overseeing the corporation's overall operations. They set business policies, monitor significant decisions, and assure compliance with laws and regulations.

Strategic Decision Making: They make crucial choices for the organization, including hiring officers, determining executive remuneration, declaring dividends, and approving significant corporate initiatives.

Fiduciary obligation: Directors bear a fiduciary obligation to act in the best interest of the company and its shareholders. This involves exerting care and loyalty and operating in good faith for the company's advantage.

Meetings and Committees: Directors attend board meetings, where they debate and vote on key company concerns. They may also serve on numerous committees, such as audit or pay committees, to monitor certain parts of the corporation.

Risk Management: Directors are accountable for analyzing and managing risks that might damage the corporation's operations, reputation, or financial stability.

Accountability: They are responsible for their actions and choices to the shareholders and must behave honestly and responsibly in their capacity as stewards of the business.

Directors have a critical role in driving the company's direction, maintaining corporate compliance, and preserving the interests of both the organization and its shareholders.

1. Officers

Officers inside an S company are responsible for the day-to-day administration and execution of the corporation's activities. Their tasks and responsibilities generally include the following:

CEO (Chief Executive Officer): The CEO is the senior executive responsible for supervising the entire operations of the organization. They formulate plans, set objectives, and work closely with other officials to guarantee the corporation's success.

COO (Chief Operating Officer): The COO controls the everyday operations of the firm. They concentrate on efficient business operations, manage resources, and develop strategies to accomplish the corporation's goals.

CFO (Chief Financial Officer): The CFO controls the financial elements of the organization. They conduct financial planning, budgeting, financial reporting, and risk management to maintain the company's financial health.

CIO/CTO (Chief Information Officer/Chief Technology Officer): The CIO or CTO is responsible for the corporation's technology requirements. They oversee IT infrastructure, digital strategy, and innovation projects to support corporate operations.

Corporate Secretary: The Corporate Secretary maintains corporate governance and regulatory compliance. They preserve records of board meetings, manage official documents, and verify compliance with legal and regulatory obligations.

Other Officers: Depending on the corporation's size and structure, additional executives like the Chief Marketing Officer, Chief HR Officer, or General Counsel can exist, each supervising their respective departments.

Officers interact with directors to execute the corporation's strategic plans, manage resources effectively, ensure compliance, and push the organization toward its objectives. They implement the policies specified by the board of directors and play a significant part in the corporation's performance.

3.2 Meetings and record-keeping obligations.

Meetings and record-keeping are key parts of maintaining an S corporation's compliance and openness. Here's an overview:

Shareholder Meetings: S businesses often host yearly shareholder meetings. These meetings are vital for analyzing business performance, choosing directors, and addressing key corporate issues. The minutes of these meetings should be preserved and maintained as part of the company records.

Board of Directors Meetings: Board meetings are conducted periodically to make crucial company decisions, evaluate financial reports, and determine strategic orientations. The minutes of these meetings should reflect discussions, resolutions, and actions taken.

Record-Keeping: S companies are expected to keep accurate and orderly company records. These comprise articles of incorporation, bylaws, meeting minutes, shareholder agreements, stock records, and financial statements. Keeping this data up-to-date guarantees compliance with legal and regulatory duties.

Financial Records: Accurate financial records must be kept to monitor revenue, spending, assets, obligations, and equity. This includes tax filings, payroll records, invoices, bank statements, and accounting ledgers.

Compliance Documents: S companies should preserve documents that indicate compliance with state and federal rules. This comprises licenses, permits, contracts, and any interaction with regulatory bodies.

Properly recorded meetings and arranged records reflect the corporation's commitment to corporate formalities, which is vital for retaining limited liability protection and guaranteeing openness among shareholders and directors.

3.3 Record-Keeping Requirements:

Record-keeping is a cornerstone of administering an S company and guaranteeing compliance with legal and regulatory duties. Here are some key record-keeping requirements:

Financial Records: Maintain thorough and accurate financial records, including income statements, balance sheets, cash flow statements, and any supporting documents linked to transactions. These records should be up-to-date and freely accessible.

Tax papers: Keep records of all tax-related papers, including filings, receipts, invoices, and any interaction with tax authorities. This covers federal, state, and local tax filings.

Employee Records: Maintain records linked to workers, such as payroll data, employment contracts, benefits information, and tax forms like W-2s and 1099s.

Corporate Governance Documents: Store all corporate governance papers, such as articles of incorporation, bylaws, meeting minutes, shareholder agreements, and board decisions.

Contracts and Agreements: Keep copies of contracts, agreements, and legal documents signed by the company, including vendor contracts, leasing agreements, and partnership agreements.

Compliance Documents: Maintain documents that indicate compliance with industry-specific legislation, licenses, permits, and any interaction with regulatory bodies.

Adhering to thorough record-keeping processes improves openness, simplifies decision-making, and helps the organization stay compliant with legal and regulatory obligations.

3.4 Maintaining conformity with state and federal regulations

Maintaining compliance with state and federal rules is vital for the effective operation of a S company. Here are some crucial elements to consider:

Tax Compliance: Adhere to tax filing dates, pay estimated taxes, and keep proper records for tax reasons. Be mindful of federal and state tax rules that apply exclusively to S companies.

Corporate Governance: Ensure compliance with corporate governance standards, including conducting regular shareholder meetings, preserving accurate meeting minutes, and adhering to the bylaws and operating agreements.

Employee Compliance: Adhere to all labor rules and regulations, including minimum wage legislation, overtime compensation, employee categorization, and workplace safety requirements.

Regulatory Compliance: Stay knowledgeable about industry-specific rules and comply with any license, certification, or permits necessary by federal or state regulatory organizations.

Financial Reporting: Prepare and submit accurate financial statements in line with generally accepted accounting principles (GAAP) and any industry-specific reporting requirements.

Data Privacy and Security: Safeguard sensitive data in conformity with data protection regulations, including appropriate management of customer information and adherence to data breach reporting obligations.

Regularly evaluate changes in laws or regulations that may impact the corporation's activities and obtain legal counsel or expert guidance to maintain continuing compliance.

CHAPTER 4

TAXATION OF S CORPORATIONS

4.1 Payroll Taxes and Employee Benefits for S Corp

The taxation of S corporation's entails factors beyond regular income tax. Payroll taxes and employee perks are significant aspects.

Payroll Taxes: S Corporations are liable for payroll taxes, including Social Security and Medicare taxes, for workers. The firm must deduct these taxes from workers' paychecks and give a commensurate amount. Owners who are also workers must pay themselves a fair remuneration subject to these taxes.

Employer Tax Responsibilities: The S Corporation is responsible for paying unemployment taxes, state and federal payroll taxes, and reporting employment taxes to the IRS.

Employee Benefits: S Corporations may provide numerous benefits to workers, such as health insurance, retirement plans (like a 401(k)), life insurance, and fringe benefits. These perks may be tax-deductible for the firm and offer substantial incentives to recruit and retain personnel.

Fringe Benefits: Some fringe benefits could be excluded from payroll taxes, such as specific educational help, employee discounts, and eligible transportation perks. Understanding which benefits qualify for tax exemptions is key.

Tax Reporting: Accurate and timely reporting of payroll taxes and employee benefits is crucial. Failure to do so might result in sanctions and legal consequences.

IRS Compliance: The business has to maintain compliance with IRS laws governing payroll taxes, such as submitting Form 941 for quarterly payroll taxes and giving workers W-2 forms.

Navigating the complexity of payroll taxes and supplying employee benefits in conformity with tax requirements is crucial for an S corporation to manage its financial obligations while providing meaningful incentives to its workers. Consulting with tax specialists or accountants helps guarantee correct tax reporting and compliance with applicable laws and regulations.

CHAPTER 5

CONVERTING TO AN S CORPORATION

5.1 Converting from a different business structure to an S corporation

Converting from another company form to an S corporation entails various processes and considerations:

Eligibility Check: Ensure the firm satisfies the eligibility criteria to elect S Corporation status. This involves having no more than 100 shareholders, people, or specified trusts or estates, and only one class of stock.

Tax Implications: Evaluate the tax consequences of the conversion. Consider prospective profits or losses, tax classification for assets, and how the change could influence the company's tax liability going forward.

Restructuring Ownership: If the organization is presently formed differently (e.g., as a C Corporation, LLC, or partnership), it could need restructuring to fulfill S Corporation rules, such as altering the number of shareholders or classes of shares.

Electing S Corporation Status: File Form 2553 with the IRS to elect S Corporation status. This document has to be filed within a particular deadline and contains facts about the company, shareholders, and the election effective date.

IRS Approval: Ensure the IRS authorizes the election. Once authorized, the S Corporation status becomes effective on the given date.

Revising Corporate Structure: Update corporation documentation, bylaws, and shareholder agreements to reflect the new S Corporation status. This can involve altering ownership percentages, stock classes, or other pertinent facts.

Compliance and Reporting: Ensure compliance with continuing S Corporation obligations, such as frequent meetings, proper record-keeping, and submitting relevant tax forms (e.g., Form 1120S for income tax).

Employee Compensation: Establish adequate remuneration for shareholders who are also workers to comply with IRS laws on salary payments.

Converting to an S corporation entails several legal, financial, and tax-related activities that require careful preparation and adherence to regulatory rules. Seeking counsel from legal and tax specialists may help negotiate the complexity and guarantee a seamless transition while leveraging the advantages of S corporation status.

5.2 Steps involved in transitioning to a S Company

Converting to an S corporation includes a set of important actions to guarantee a flawless transition:

Eligibility Assessment: Determine whether the firm fits the S Corporation standards, including having less than 100 shareholders, U.S. residency, and a single class of stock.

Review Tax Implications: Understand the tax effects of the conversion. Assess possible tax bills, capital gains, and other financial implications related to the change in status.

Evaluate Corporate Structure: Review the present company structure (e.g., C Corporation, LLC, or partnership) to determine essential adjustments for S Corporation eligibility, such as restructuring ownership and classes of shares.

Document Preparation: Prepare appropriate documentation, including company bylaws, articles of formation, and shareholder agreements that match S Corporation regulations.

File Form 2553: Complete and submit Form 2553 (Election by a Small Business Corporation) with the IRS. Ensure all relevant information, such as corporate data and shareholder permission, is appropriately delivered.

IRS Approval: Await confirmation from the IRS about the approval of the S Corporation election. The IRS will check whether the company qualifies and authorizes the election's effective date.

Notification to Stakeholders: Inform shareholders and stakeholders of the decision to convert to a S corporation. Communicate changes in ownership structure, voting rights, and other important facts.

Update Legal Documents: Amend business documentation and agreements to reflect the new S Corporation status. Ensure alignment with the IRS-approved election.

Compliance and Ongoing Requirements: Establish processes to comply with S Corporation duties, including frequent meetings, preserving documents, and following IRS standards for tax filings.

Review Employee Compensation: Ensure that remuneration for shareholder-employees complies with reasonable criteria to fulfill IRS rules.

Each stage in the conversion process demands careful attention to detail and respect for regulatory regulations. Seeking professional counsel from legal and financial specialists may speed the conversion process and help negotiate any complications.

CHAPTER 6

SINGLE OWNER S CORP PAYROLL BASICS

Understanding payroll for a single-owner S corporation includes unique considerations:

Owner-Employee Classification: As the only owner of an S corporation, it's vital to decide the appropriate compensation for yourself as an employee. The IRS demands that shareholder-employees get adequate pay for their efforts.

Reasonable Salary Determination: Assess your tasks, responsibilities, and industry norms to determine an acceptable salary. This wage should represent what you'd pay an unaffiliated party for equivalent services in the same business setting.

Payroll Processing: Implement a payroll system to handle salary payments, tax withholdings, and other payroll-related tasks. Ensure compliance with federal and state payroll tax rules.

Taxation on Salary: Understand the tax consequences of your compensation. While earnings are subject to income tax, they're also liable for Social Security and Medicare taxes. Other profits from the firm may not be subject to these taxes.

Filing Requirements: File payroll tax returns and guarantee timely payment of employment taxes. This comprises Form 941 (the employer's quarterly federal tax return) and Form W-2 (the wage and tax statement).

Record-Keeping: Maintain accurate records of payroll transactions, including salaries, withholdings, and tax payments. These documents are necessary for audits and compliance reasons.

Consult professionals: Engage with an accountant or tax specialist to negotiate complicated tax laws, maintain correct payroll processing, and maximize tax strategies while keeping compliance with IRS requirements.

Employee Benefits: Evaluate and develop any extra perks or compensations beyond the pay, examining their tax effects and how they correspond with S Corporation requirements.

Regular Reviews: Periodically evaluate and modify your remuneration to reflect changes in your job, responsibilities, or market standards. This assures continuous compliance with the IRS's requirement of fair pay.

Operating as a single-owner S Corporation requires a firm grasp of payroll essentials, including the assessment of appropriate compensation and tax liabilities and adherence to reporting and filing standards. Consulting with financial specialists may provide helpful counsel tailored to your unique position and assure compliance with legislation.

6.1 Missteps in Single-Owner S Corp Payroll

In managing payroll for a single-owner S Corporation, various errors may occur:

Unreasonable Compensation: Not paying oneself suitable compensation as the owner-employee. This may draw an IRS inspection, leading to fines and tax ramifications.

Failing to Separate Personal and Business Expenses: Mixing personal and business expenses may complicate payroll administration and can generate complications during IRS audits.

Improper Tax Withholdings: Failing to withhold the right amount of federal and state taxes from your paycheck may lead to fines or tax underpayment.

Non-Compliance with Reporting Requirements: Missing deadlines or improperly reporting payroll tax forms, such as Form 941, or W-2s, may result in fines and compliance concerns.

Inadequate Record-Keeping: Poor documentation of payroll-related activities, including salary payments, tax withholdings, and files, may lead to mistakes or non-compliance during audits.

Ignoring Quarterly Tax Deposits: Not remitting payroll taxes quarterly may result in fines and interest charges, hurting the financial sustainability of the firm.

Misclassifying Workers: Incorrectly classifying workers as independent contractors instead of employees may lead to misreported income and IRS fines.

Overlooking Employment Tax Obligations: S corporations must pay and report employment taxes appropriately, including Social Security, Medicare, and federal unemployment taxes.

Failing to Adjust Compensation: Not evaluating and revising the owner-employee's remuneration often to reflect market changes, company performance, or changes in duties and responsibilities.

Lack of Professional Guidance: Failing to obtain assistance from tax specialists or accountants may lead to problems in payroll processing and compliance.

Understanding and avoiding these blunders is crucial for a single-owner S corporation to guarantee compliance with IRS requirements, keep correct financial records, and limit possible fines or legal concerns linked with payroll administration. Consulting specialists may help manage these intricacies and guarantee appropriate payroll processes.

CHAPTER 7

EXPLORING ALTERNATIVES TO THE S CORPORATION STRUCTURE

7.1 Limited Liability Company (LLC)

Absolutely. When investigating alternatives to the S Corporation form, one notable entity to examine is the Limited Liability Company (LLC). LLCs provide a versatile company form, combining the liability protection of a corporation with the tax benefits of a partnership or sole proprietorship.

An LLC safeguards its owners from personal responsibility for commercial debts or legal proceedings taken against the organization. It also provides for a more adjustable management structure compared to corporations, offering alternatives for member-managed or manager-managed models.

Regarding taxes, LLCs provide pass-through taxation, meaning the income and losses of the firm flow through to the owners' tax returns, avoiding double taxation that may occur with C corporations. This taxation arrangement generally results in simplified tax forms.

Moreover, LLCs don't have the same rigid obligations for meetings and record-keeping as corporations, delivering a more relaxed administrative load.

LLCs allow for a varied spectrum of ownership. They may have an infinite number of members and can incorporate other LLCs, corporations, non-US residents, or trusts as members, providing tremendous flexibility in arranging ownership.

Despite these advantages, LLCs may not be suited for every firm. The eligibility and operating criteria might differ by state, thereby altering the entity's efficiency depending on the business's demands. When assessing whether an LLC is the proper option for an S corporation, firms should carefully evaluate the operational, tax, and liability consequences to guarantee alignment with their long-term objectives and requirements.

7.2 C Corporation

Certainly. When researching alternatives to the S Corporation form, the C Corporation (C Corp) is another notable entity worth studying. C corporations differ substantially from S corporations in numerous crucial areas.

Firstly, C corporations are independent legal entities apart from their owners, offering limited liability protection to stockholders. This implies that stockholders normally aren't personally accountable for the corporation's debts or legal proceedings taken against the firm, safeguarding personal assets from business-related obligations.

One of the primary distinctions between C corporations and S corporation's rests on taxes. Corporations are subject to double taxation: the business itself is taxed on its earnings, and shareholders are taxed on dividends or distributions received from the corporation. This double taxation might occasionally result in greater total tax payments.

However, C Corporations have several features that can attract firms, such as the opportunity to attract investors via the sale of stock and the lack of limits on the number of shareholders or the citizenship status of owners, unlike S Corporations.

Additionally, C corporations have greater latitude in constructing employee benefit programs, including giving a larger choice of deductible fringe benefits.

On the negative side, C corporations have extra formality and administrative duties. These may include conducting frequent shareholder meetings, keeping accurate records, and following specified corporate formalities to ensure restricted liability protections.

Deciding between an S corporation and a C corporation includes assessing the business's particular requirements, future objectives, and tax ramifications. While C corporations provide significant benefits, the decision ultimately rests on issues including taxation preferences, development methods, and long-term ambitions.

7.3 Partnership

Partnerships provide another option for the S Corporation form. They vary greatly in terms of formation, responsibility, and taxes.

A partnership is a company organization created by two or more people who share ownership and operational duties. Unlike corporations, partnerships do not constitute independent legal bodies. There are several sorts of partnerships:

General Partnerships: In this model, partners participate equally in earnings, losses, and managerial duties. They also share limitless accountability for the business's debts and liabilities.

Limited Partnerships: Limited partnerships consist of general partners, who operate the firm and have unlimited responsibility, and limited partners, who invest but have limited liability and are not engaged in daily operations.

Limited Liability Partnerships (LLPs): These partnerships give limited responsibility to all partners, insulating them from certain obligations originating from the conduct of other partners or employees.

Partnerships are taxed differently than corporations. They are considered pass-through businesses, meaning income and losses travel through the firm to the partners, who record them on their tax returns. This eliminates the problem of double taxes posed by C corporations.

While partnerships provide ease in their creation and operating structure, they lack the legal protections given by corporations. Partners in a general partnership, for example, have personal accountability for the partnership's debts and obligations, which might expose their assets to hazards linked to the firm.

corporation Deciding between a S Corporation and a partnership relies on numerous aspects, including liability issues, tax considerations, ownership structure, and the amount of control and management required by the owners. Each structure has its benefits and downsides; therefore, it's vital to measure them against the unique demands and objectives of the organization.

7.4 Sole Proprietorship

A sole proprietorship is the simplest and most prevalent kind of company organization, owned and run by a single person. It's an unincorporated business with the owner keeping total control over operations, earnings, and decision-making.

Key features of a single proprietorship include:

Ownership: The firm is wholly owned by one individual who undertakes all responsibility and liabilities. There's no legal separation between the owner and the company entity.

culpability: The proprietor carries limitless personal culpability for the business's debts and legal responsibilities. This implies personal assets are at risk of being used to pay any company-related obligations, which is a big negative compared to alternative business arrangements like corporations or LLCs.

Taxation: Like partnerships, sole proprietorships are considered pass-through companies for tax reasons. The owner declares company earnings and losses on their tax return (Form 1040) and pays taxes depending on individual income tax rates. There's no separate business tax return necessary, simplifying tax filings.

Flexibility: Sole proprietorships are straightforward and cheap to start and dissolve. They give ultimate control over decision-making and company operations without the need for complicated corporate formalities or governance structures.

However, because of the direct liability exposure, sole proprietorships may not be ideal for enterprises with high-risk operations or considerable liabilities. Additionally, they might experience issues obtaining funds or recruiting investments since the structure does not distribute shares to prospective investors or partners.

Choosing between an S corporation and a sole proprietorship requires careful consideration of aspects such as personal responsibility, tax ramifications, growth possibilities, and long-term company objectives. Each structure has various benefits and drawbacks, and the selection should coincide with the individual demands and circumstances of the company owner.

Reid C. Williams

THE ULTIMATE LLC AND S-CORPORATION BEGINNER'S GUIDE

CHAPTER 8

DISSOLVING AN S CORPORATION

8.1 Reasons for Dissolving a S Company.

Dissolving an S corporation is a serious decision, sometimes caused by several reasons:

Company Closure: If the company has fulfilled its function or no longer corresponds with the owner's aims, dissolution can be the proper option. This might be due to retirement, a change in professional path, or accomplishing the basic goals established for the organization.

Financial Challenges: Financial bankruptcy or the inability to maintain operations owing to market circumstances, economic downturns, or unanticipated obligations may lead to dissolution.

Ownership Changes: Disputes among shareholders or the departure of important players could start the dissolution process. Incompatibility in vision or strategy among the company's leadership may also be an issue.

Statutory Requirements: Regulatory changes or an inability to comply with state or federal laws could necessitate dissolution. Non-compliance with filing requirements, tax duties, or maintaining corporate formalities might lead to legal issues.

Merger or Acquisition: If the firm merges with another business organization or is bought by a bigger corporation, dissolution of the S Corporation can occur.

Loss of S Corporation Status: If the firm fails to fulfill the eligibility conditions for S Corporation status, such as surpassing the maximum number of shareholders, it could lead to dissolution.

Dissolving an S corporation is a formal process that differs based on state laws and the company's internal processes. It often entails a vote by the shareholders, submitting dissolution paperwork with the state, resolving outstanding liabilities, and dividing assets among owners as per the company's bylaws or agreements. Additionally, the IRS and state taxation authorities should be informed of the dissolution, and final tax returns need to be submitted.

It's vital to follow the right legal processes when dissolving an S corporation to guarantee compliance with all legal requirements, avoid possible liabilities, and properly finish the business activities. Seeking legal and financial counsel is suggested to manage the dissolution process effectively and safeguard the interests of all parties involved.

8.2 Process for dissolving an S company.

Dissolving an S corporation includes an organized procedure to lawfully cease its activities. Here's an overview of the stages normally involved:

Board Resolution: The board of directors convenes a meeting to recommend the dissolution and approves a resolution to dissolve the company. This resolution should be noted in the corporate minutes.

Shareholder Vote: Shareholders must vote on the decision to dissolve the S Corporation. The decision can require a majority or supermajority vote, as provided in the corporation's bylaws or operating agreements.

Filing Dissolution Documents: File dissolution documents with the state where the S Corporation was initially established. This normally entails filing articles or a certificate of dissolution explaining the decision to dissolve the company. Compliance with state requirements for dissolution filings is vital.

Notify Creditors and Settle Debts: Notify creditors and settle outstanding debts and obligations. This involves paying off creditors, settling ongoing disputes, and satisfying contractual commitments. This phase guarantees that the corporation's financial issues are suitably resolved.

Asset Distribution: If any assets remain after resolving debts, they are divided among the shareholders according to their ownership interests, as defined in the company's bylaws or operating agreements.

Tax Filings and Final Returns: File final federal, state, and local tax returns for the S Corporation. Ensure all tax responsibilities are satisfied, including payroll taxes, income taxes, and any other mandatory filings. Obtain appropriate tax clearance or certifications from tax authorities.

Employee Notifications: If the S Corporation has workers, present them with notice of closure, pay their salaries, benefits, and other entitlements, and conform to employment termination requirements.

Cancel Permits & Licenses: Cancel all business permits, licenses, or registrations related to the S Corporation. This includes federal employment identification numbers (EINs) and state-specific permits.

Notify Authorities: Inform the Internal Revenue Service (IRS) and state authorities of the dissolution. This assures compliance with tax requirements and prevents future liabilities or fines.

Publication of Dissolution: Some states could require a notice of dissolution to be published in a local newspaper to alert creditors and other interested parties.

Dissolving a S corporation necessitates respect for legal regulations, which may differ among states. It's important to acquire legal advice or speak with a certified public accountant (CPA) well-versed in corporation dissolution to guarantee compliance with all relevant stages and laws. This helps protect against any legal complications and enables a smooth closure of the business's activities.

8.3 Tax ramifications of terminating an S company.

The dissolution of an S corporation includes various tax repercussions that business owners should consider. Here are some significant tax factors to keep in mind:

Final Tax Returns: Once the decision to dissolve an S corporation is taken, the corporation must submit a final tax return. This contains IRS Form 1120S, which covers the time from the commencement of the tax year until the date of dissolution. Ensure that all income, deductions, and credits are appropriately recorded.

Tax Clearance: Before concluding the dissolution, seek tax clearance or a certificate from the IRS and state tax authorities. This guarantees that all tax payments are addressed, limiting the possibility of future tax concerns for both the firm and its shareholders.

Distribution of Assets: When assets are disbursed to shareholders as part of the dissolution, this might have tax ramifications. Certain assets may have risen in value, resulting in capital gains taxes on shareholders upon delivery. Ensure correct valuation and tax planning for these payouts.

Cancellation of Debt: If the company cancels any debts after dissolution, this can cause cancellation of debt (COD) income, subject to taxes. Shareholders could be accountable for declaring this as income on their tax filings.

Liquidation Gain or Loss: The company can suffer a gain or loss on the sale or distribution of its assets following dissolution. This might have capital gains or ordinary income tax consequences, which are passed on to the shareholders.

Employment Taxes: Ensure that all employment taxes, including payroll taxes, are completely paid. Unpaid payroll taxes may lead to personal responsibility for the corporation's officials or accountable parties.

State and Local Taxes: Different states have varying tax regulations addressing company dissolution. Comply with state regulations for tax filings, including final state tax reports, asset disposal, and tax clearance.

Tax Elections: Depending on the circumstances, the S Corporation could need to make different tax elections or changes as part of the dissolution procedure. This might involve invalidating past tax elections or forming new ones depending on the dissolution's structure.

These tax effects underline the significance of proper preparation and compliance with tax legislation when dissolving an S Corporation. Seeking counsel from tax specialists or financial consultants may help negotiate these difficulties and avoid tax obligations throughout the divorce process.

8.4 Types of S.corp to Dissolve

Dissolving a S Corporation may occur via different routes, each having its repercussions. Here are many forms of dissolution:

Voluntary Dissolution: This is a planned dissolution undertaken by the corporation's shareholders or directors. It often entails submitting dissolution documents to the state, resolving debts, distributing assets to shareholders, and legally terminating the firm.

Involuntary Dissolution: This is forced dissolution imposed by external forces, such as court orders, regulatory infractions, or failure to comply with state or federal standards. It may also come from shareholder conflicts or financial difficulty, leading to legal measures that require the dissolution of the organization.

Administrative Dissolution: If a S business fails to satisfy certain state duties (e.g., submitting yearly reports, paying taxes or fees), the state may administratively dissolve the business without judicial intervention. This dissolution isn't at the corporation's desire and happens due to non-compliance.

Judicial Dissolution: This dissolution happens by a court order in response to a petition submitted by a shareholder, director, or creditor. Reasons for pursuing judicial dissolution might include impasse among shareholders, fraudulent actions, or oppressive conduct by the corporation's leadership.

Short-Form Dissolution: Some states provide a simpler dissolution procedure for businesses with minor assets and no ongoing debts or commitments. This rapid dissolution procedure may not involve official shareholder meetings or lengthy documentation.

Each form of disintegration has specific procedures and ramifications. Voluntary dissolutions often enable greater control and planning, whereas involuntary or judicial dissolutions sometimes require legal actions and may result in undesirable consequences for the organization and its stakeholders. Understanding the various processes and legal repercussions connected with each kind is vital when contemplating the dissolution of an S Corporation. Seeking legal counsel or expert guidance may help negotiate these obstacles and guarantee a seamless dissolution procedure.

CHAPTER 9

THE DOCUMENTS YOU NEED TO CREATE AN S. CORP

Establishing a S Corporation involves numerous crucial papers to assure compliance and correct creation. These documents include:

Articles of Incorporation: This fundamental document provides crucial characteristics about the organization, such as its name, location, purpose, registered agent, and the number and kinds of shares to be issued. It is filed with the state's Secretary of State or comparable entity.

Corporate Bylaws: Bylaws serve as the corporation's internal rulebook, detailing how the organization will run. They include processes for shareholder and board meetings, officer positions, voting rights, and other operational norms.

Shareholder Agreement: This agreement delineates the rights and duties of shareholders, including things such as stock ownership, transfer limitations, buy-sell clauses, and dispute resolution processes.

Meeting Minutes: Detailed records of shareholder and director meetings, including resolutions, decisions, and debates, are vital for legal compliance and preserving corporate formality.

Employer Identification Number (EIN): An EIN, issued by the IRS, acts as the corporation's unique identification number for tax reasons and is important for employing workers and creating bank accounts.
S company Election Form: Form 2553, filed to the IRS, authorizes the company to elect the S Corporation tax classification. This form is necessary to be taxed as a S Corporation rather than a C Corporation.
Stock Certificates: These certificates establish the ownership of shares in the firm and contain facts such as shareholder names, the number of shares, and the share class.
Financial Statements and Tax Filings: The company should keep accurate financial records, including income statements, balance sheets, and tax filings to comply with federal and state tax regulations.
Operating Agreements (if applicable): While not obligatory for S Corporations, an operating agreement might be needed in certain states to provide internal governance for single-member LLCs or multi-member LLCs adopting S Corporation taxation.
These agreements serve as the legal basis and structure for the S Corporation, assuring legal conformity, identifying rights and obligations, and offering directions for operation. It's vital to write these agreements thoroughly and frequently with the aid of legal or

financial specialists to fulfill particular state regulations and safeguard the corporation's interests.

CHAPTER 10

PRACTICAL TIPS AND COMMON MISTAKES TO AVOID

10,1 Practical tips

Practical suggestions for operating a S Corporation effectively:

Stay Compliant: Keep up with state and federal rules, filing requirements, and tax responsibilities to retain the corporation's good standing.

Regular Meetings: Conduct regular shareholder and director meetings to discuss business concerns, record minutes, and make crucial decisions for the company's future.

Financial Transparency: Maintain accurate financial records and separate personal and corporate funds to guarantee transparency and compliance.

Seek Professional Advice: Consult with lawyers, accountants, or financial consultants knowledgeable in company concerns to understand complicated challenges and make educated choices.

Risk Management: Implement techniques to manage risks, such as liability insurance, contracts, and legal safeguards, to secure the corporation's assets.

Tax Planning: Optimize tax tactics by knowing S Corporation's tax advantages and contacting tax specialists for effective tax planning.

Document Everything: Maintain comprehensive records of company activity, contracts, agreements, and significant decisions to provide legal protection and transparency.

Regular Updates: Periodically examine and amend business papers, bylaws, and agreements to adapt to changing conditions and stay compliant.

Employee Relations: Implement fair and transparent employment regulations, give employees perks, and create a good working atmosphere to retain talent.

Future Planning: Develop a strategy plan defining the corporation's long-term objectives, expansion strategies, and succession plans for sustainable development.

These ideas may assist S Corporations in negotiating the complexity of corporate administration, guaranteeing compliance, transparency, and strategic development while avoiding frequent mistakes. Additionally, obtaining expert help when appropriate may give vital insights for optimal operations.

10.2 Common Mistakes to Avoid

Some frequent pitfalls to avoid while operating a S Corporation:

Neglecting Compliance: Failing to conform to state and federal standards, skipping files, or disregarding tax duties may lead to fines and legal troubles.

Improper Record Keeping: Inadequate or incorrect financial records, including not segregating personal and corporate money, may result in confusion, compliance concerns, and legal obligations.

Lack of Corporate Formalities: Failure to conduct regular meetings, retain meeting minutes, or maintain clear corporate rules could threaten the corporation's standing and legal protection.

Misclassification of Employees: Incorrectly categorizing people as independent contractors rather than employees may lead to tax and legal penalties.

Inadequate Insurance Coverage: Insufficient liability insurance or not having the correct coverage could expose the business to risks in case of legal claims or unforeseen incidents.

Ignoring Tax Planning: Not utilizing potential tax benefits or neglecting to prepare for taxes adequately may lead to lost opportunities and greater tax bills.

Disregarding Professional counsel: Avoiding legal, financial, or tax counsel from skilled professionals could result in making misinformed judgments or missing key insights.

Mixing Personal and Business Affairs: Blurring the distinctions between personal and business finances may damage the corporation's legal protection and generate tax issues.

Failure to Update papers: Neglecting to update business papers, such as bylaws, agreements, or operating procedures, could lead to obsolete practices or non-compliance.

Overlooking Succession Planning: Not having a clear strategy for leadership transitions or company continuity may generate instability during changes in management or unanticipated circumstances.

By avoiding these typical errors, S Corporations may maintain compliance, preserve their assets, and create sustainable development while limiting risks and legal difficulties. Seeking expert assistance and sticking to best practices may considerably help the corporation's long-term development.

CONCLUSION

In the evolving world of company formations, both Limited Liability Companies (LLCs) and S Corporations provide significant benefits and considerations for entrepreneurs and business owners. Understanding the subtleties and requirements of funding, controlling, and dissolving these organizations is vital for making educated choices that correspond with particular company objectives.

Throughout this thorough tutorial, we've dived into the deep aspects of LLCs and S Corporations. From illuminating the basic ideas to navigating the procedural subtleties, each chapter sought to give thorough knowledge to individuals commencing on their entrepreneurial path or wanting to reorganize their corporate organizations.

The LLC part covers everything from the core knowledge of what an LLC includes to the complexities of its creation, administration, possible problems, and conversion procedures. Detailed insights into accounting, taxes, and dissolution were presented to empower readers with practical understanding.

In the ensuing section on S Corporations, we investigated the specificities of forming, administering, and converting to a S Corporation. The booklet provides a detailed overview of the duties and obligations, tax consequences, dissolution methods, and alternatives.

By stressing the advantages, downsides, procedural intricacies, and possible errors, this book sought to provide readers with a wealth of information to make well-informed judgments matched with their company goals.

In conclusion, the route to choosing and operating the most appropriate business structure comprises a plethora of issues, and this book serves as a thorough roadmap for anyone navigating the difficult terrain of LLCs and S Corporations. By incorporating a comprehensive awareness of these entities' complexities, readers are better able to make strategic choices that connect with their entrepreneurial objectives and support long-term economic success.

www.ingramcontent.com/pod-product-compliance
Lightning Source LLC
Chambersburg PA
CBHW071202290526
45796CB00008B/110
9798875561733